Whittling
ON THE GO

Whittling
ON THE GO

13 EASY-TO-LEARN WOODCARVING PROJECTS

DAVID YOUNG

© 2025 by David Young and Fox Chapel Publishing Company, Inc.

Whittling on the Go is an original work, first published in 2025 by Fox Chapel Publishing Company, Inc. The patterns contained herein are copyrighted by the author. Readers may make copies of these patterns for personal use. The patterns themselves, however, are not to be duplicated for resale or distribution under any circumstances. Any such copying is a violation of copyright law.

All rights reserved. No part of this publication may be reproduced, stored in a retrieval system or transmitted, in any form or by any means, electronic, mechanical, photocopying, recording or otherwise, without the prior written permission of the copyright holders.

ISBN 978-1-4971-0476-1

The Cataloging-in-Publication Data is on file with the Library of Congress.

Managing Editor: Gretchen Bacon
Acquisitions Editor: Kaylee J. Schofield
Editor: Joseph Borden
Designer: Freire SL
Proofreader: Kelly Umenhofer

To learn more about the other great books from Fox Chapel Publishing, or to find a retailer near you, call toll-free at 800-457-9112 or visit us at *www.FoxChapelPublishing.com*.
You can also send mail to:
Fox Chapel Publishing
903 Square Street
Mount Joy, PA 17552

We are always looking for talented authors. To submit an idea, please send a brief inquiry to acquisitions@foxchapelpublishing.com.

Printed in China
First printing

Because working with knives and other tools inherently includes the risk of injury and damage, this book cannot guarantee that creating the projects in this book is safe for everyone. For this reason, this book is sold without warranties or guarantees of any kind, expressed or implied, and the publisher and the author disclaim any liability for any injuries, losses, or damages caused in any way by the content of this book or the reader's use of the tools needed to complete the projects presented here. The publisher and the author urge all readers to thoroughly review each project and to understand the use of all tools before beginning any project.

Introduction

The idea of whittling as a hobby first occurred to me while on a family vacation in the summer of 2018. I spent an afternoon sitting by a campfire, whittling personalized marshmallow sticks for my kids. When I got home, I realized that had been one of the most relaxing and enjoyable parts of the trip. Hoping to recapture that moment, I bought a block of carving wood from a local hardware store. It sat in my garage untouched for six months until, one night, I stumbled upon a Doug Linker video on YouTube. Inspired, I grabbed a knife—that was definitely not intended for carving—and stayed up late into the night working on the largest five-minute wizard you have ever seen, cutting my finger pretty badly in the process. The carving wasn't pretty (and neither was my finger), but I was hooked.

I remember those early days of carving well. After quickly acquiring a carving glove and a dedicated whittling knife, I started digging into whatever resources I could find—online videos, magazines, books—and learning everything I could about woodcarving. As a beginner, I quickly came to two realizations. First, in order to get better at whittling, I was going to need to learn some additional skills I hadn't initially considered, namely, sharpening, painting, and finishing. Second, there are about as many opinions on how to carve, sharpen, paint, and finish as there are carvers.

To some extent, every new carver needs to wade through different approaches and opinions, try different things, and learn what works for them. This applies to everything, from choosing a knife to sharpening, painting, and even developing your own carving style. Even so, I think there is something to be said for keeping things as simple as possible for beginners. What you will find in this book is not a comprehensive guide to woodcarving, but the basic information and advice that worked for me and that I believe will be helpful for a beginner to get started. That said, I encourage you to supplement my advice and recommendations with a healthy dose of your own experience and other resources to find what works for you.

My focus in this book is on what I would call "hobby whittling" or "craft whittling," which I define as using knives that are specifically made for whittling and wood that is specifically intended for carving. While there are all kinds of approaches to woodcarving, the complete beginner will benefit from the simplicity of starting with a nice sharp knife and a good soft piece of wood.

With all of this in mind, I have three goals that I hope to accomplish in this book.

1. I want to introduce whittling to complete beginners. I will assume that you are completely new to woodcarving and explain all of the terms and techniques that you need to get started. The first four projects, in particular, are specifically designed to gradually introduce cuts and develop basic skills, preparing you to take on the projects in the rest of the book. Additionally, all of the projects use small blocks of wood in easy-to-find sizes, with no need for power saws or other special equipment.

2. I want to provide projects that are attainable for beginners but also fun and engaging for experienced carvers. The projects in this book are generally pretty simple and fast. As you progress, you will find that the patterns and shapes remain fairly simple, but gradually increase in challenge and difficulty. More experienced carvers should find satisfaction in executing these designs cleanly and precisely, but will also find plenty of opportunities to customize and add their own variations to these designs.

3. I want to provide small, portable projects that you can take with you on the go. Part of the appeal of whittling is that you don't need a lot of special materials or equipment. Everything you need to work on these projects can be packed in a small bag or large pocket so that you will be ready to whittle anywhere.

Whether this book marks the beginning of your journey into the world of whittling and woodcarving, or you are an experienced carver looking for some fun, simple projects, I hope you enjoy the projects and information provided in this book. Have fun and happy whittling!

-DAVID YOUNG

For Katie, my greatest encourager and supporter.

For Ben, Joanna, and Noelle, my most avid collectors and critics.

Table of Contents

Getting Started

Introduction to Wood 8

Choosing a Knife 9

Other Materials and Tools 11

Sharpening 13

Safety.......................... 17

The Basic Cuts of Whittling 18

Painting and Finishing

Painting........................ 20

Antiquing and Dry-Brushing...... 26

Finishing....................... 28

Adding Accessories.............. 31

Projects

Whittle People 34

Simple Cactus. 40

Hatching Chicks. 46

Simple Wood Spirit. 56

Alligator 62

Goldfish 68

Seashell. 74

Grumpy (or Happy) Cat 80

Super Simple Gnomes 88

Butterfly 94

Pineapple 102

Rose in Vase. 110

Old Man in Wood. 118

Index 126

About the Author 128

Getting Started

One of the great things about whittling as a hobby is that it doesn't require a lot of equipment to get started. In addition to a knife and some wood, you need just a few things to keep your knife sharp and use it safely. In this chapter, I will provide a quick summary of what you need to start whittling and prepare you to take on the projects in the remainder of the book.

It is important to have basic whittling kit that includes your carving knife, measuring tools, sharpening tools, and carving safety gear before you make your first cut.

Introduction to Wood

Let's start by looking at what you need most to whittle: a good piece of wood.

Selecting Wood

The best wood for beginners and the wood most commonly used for carving is basswood (known as linden or limewood in Europe). Basswood is a soft hardwood with a tight, even grain that holds details well. In the US, there are two types of basswood: northern basswood and southern basswood. Northern basswood tends to be very light in color and is very easy to carve. Southern basswood tends to be darker and can sometimes be a little harder to carve, though still usable. When selecting a specific piece of wood, look for straight, even grain without any blemishes or knots.

If you can't find any basswood, other commonly used woods include butternut, birch, ash, pine, and poplar. Woods like walnut or cherry can be desirable for their color, but they are harder, more brittle, and more difficult for a beginner to carve.

Basswood blocks of various sizes. The two blocks on the left are southern basswood and have a slightly darker color than the rest, which are northern basswood.

Understanding Wood Grain

The grain in this wood is horizontal. The pencil lines indicate the direction to make "downhill" cuts with the grain.

As you carve, it's important to pay attention to the direction of the wood grain and understand when you are carving with, across, or against the grain.

When making cuts parallel to the direction of the grain, you are carving **with** the grain. When making cuts perpendicular to the grain, you are carving **across/against** the grain. In practice, many cuts will be made at different angles, which can be done either with or against the grain. The simplest way to identify if a cut is with or against the grain is to hold your carving so that the grain is horizontal, and then identify if the cut will be downhill or uphill. If carving downhill, you are carving with the grain, but if carving uphill, you are carving against the grain. Just remember, it's always easier to carve downhill than uphill.

Although it is good to carve with the grain whenever you can, it is possible (and sometimes necessary) to carve across or against the grain. When carving across or against the grain, use the widest part of your blade and start with small cuts to avoid breaking the wood. If you are doing a lot of across or against the grain cuts, consider stropping before and/or after doing so (see page 14).

Choosing a Knife

Woodcarving knives come in all shapes and sizes that serve many different purposes. If you are just getting into whittling, choosing your first knife can be a little overwhelming. The information below is intended to provide some guidelines for beginners on what to look for in a good all-around carving knife. A knife that meets the criteria below will work well for the projects in this book and serve you well for many years to come. As you continue to carve, you will develop your own preferences and start to identify other types of knives that you may find useful.

- **Length.** A blade that is 1 ½" to 2" (3.8 to 5.1cm) long makes for a good all-around carving knife. Knives in this range are capable of making both roughing cuts as well as detail cuts.
- **Thickness.** One of the distinguishing characteristics of whittling knives is that they tend to be very thin. The thicker the blade, the more difficult it will be to push through a piece of wood, and the more likely it will be to split the wood apart rather than cutting cleanly. A blade thickness of ⅟₃₂" to ⅟₁₆" (1 to 2mm) or even less should work well for the type of whittling covered in this book.
- **Cutting edge.** For most beginners, a straight cutting edge is easiest to start with. While curved edges are helpful for some applications, the straight blade makes it very easy to pinpoint the location of the cutting edge and tip, allowing for greater precision and control. A straight cutting edge also makes sharpening very easy.

Preparing Wood

Even generally soft wood can sometimes become overly hard and difficult to carve. Whether it is due to age, variations between trees, overly dry climate, or some other factor, there are a couple tricks carvers will use to soften up their wood. A common approach is to spray a 50⁄50 mixture of water and rubbing alcohol onto the wood prior to carving. Another is to store wood in an airtight container with a damp cloth (not touching the wood) for a day or two prior to carving. Keep in mind that these are last-minute options to apply before carving. You should store your wood in a cool, dry place. If you have ongoing problems with hard wood, you might try other sources or types of wood as a point of comparison.

These knives are all different, but they are each good choices for an all-around carving knife.

- **Detail tip.** If you are starting with one knife, you will want to make sure the tip is shaped well for carving fine details. The tip should come down to a point at the front of the knife, and the thickness of the blade should also decrease as it nears the tip. An overly rounded or thick tip will make carving fine details more difficult.
- **Grind.** The grind of the blade refers to the shape of the sides of the blade as they come down to form the cutting edge. A flat-ground blade is generally recommended for beginners and makes sharpening especially easy. A flat grind means that the sides of the blade are completely flat as they come down from the spine to the cutting edge. Other grinds you may find on whittling knives include the scandi (short for Scandinavian) grind, in which the angle toward the cutting edge starts farther down on the blade, or the convex grind, in which the sides curve down to the cutting edge.
- **Blade material.** A good whittling knife will have a high-carbon steel blade. Many pocketknives are made from stainless steel, which is great for overall strength and corrosion resistance, but makes them more difficult to sharpen and maintain.
- **Handle.** Handle shape is a matter of personal preference, and it may be hard to know what you prefer as a beginner. If possible, try to hold a knife before you buy it. If that's not possible, then you may want to start with more generic rectangular or oval handles, which tend to be usable for most people.

Blade Grinds

Flat

Scandi

Convex

Depending on your carving experience and skill, you will have to decide what blade grinds (flat, scandi, or convex) work best for you when choosing whittling knives.

- **Folding knives.** Most pocketknives don't have the right blade shape, grind, and/or steel to be ideal for the type of whittling taught in this book. Additionally, the handles tend to be less comfortable for longer whittling sessions. However, if you would still prefer a folding knife, it is possible to find some that meet the criteria described above, and a few manufacturers make folding blades that are specifically designed for whittling.

The Rockwell Hardness Scale for Steel

Steel hardness is commonly measured by a rating system called the Rockwell Hardness Scale. Not all manufacturers advertise the Rockwell hardness of their blades, but most of the reputable knife makers do. For whittling, you want a knife that is hard enough to hold an edge, but soft enough that you can easily sharpen it. Whittling knives generally fall in the range of 58 to 62 on the Rockwell Hardness Scale.

Other Materials and Tools

Tools, such as V-tools and U-gouges, can help add texture and detail to your carving projects.

In addition to knives, there are a few other tools and pieces of equipment that you may find helpful as you begin your carving journey.

V-Tools

After a knife, one of the first tools that most carvers acquire is a V-tool. Sometimes referred to as a V-gouge or V-parting tool, the V-tool is made up of two forward-facing cutting edges

Whittling or Woodcarving?

It's common to hear the words "whittling" and "woodcarving" used interchangeably, which might have you wondering if there is any difference. In general, "woodcarving" is a broad term that includes a wide range of styles and methods for carving wood. Although there is no formally agreed upon definition for "whittling," it is commonly used to refer to woodcarving with just a knife. So when you are whittling, you are woodcarving. Based on this definition, the projects in this book are almost entirely whittling projects, but we will use some extra tools on a few projects that take them into the more general realm of woodcarving.

that come together in a V shape. When pushed through wood, it quickly makes clean and even V-shaped cuts. V-tools are classified based on their width and the angle of their V. For example, a ¼" (6mm) 60-degree V-tool or a ⅛" (3mm) 90-degree V-tool. The Simple Wood Spirit project in this book is specifically designed to introduce and provide lots of practice with using a V-tool.

Gouges

Gouges are a broad category of carving tools that have forward-facing edges and push directly through wood. Gouges generally have a curved cutting edge and are categorized based on the depth of their curve on a scale from 1 to 11. A #1 gouge is completely flat and is more commonly referred to as a chisel. A #3 gouge has a very shallow curve, whereas a #5 gouge has a medium

V-tools easily make clean and even V-cuts, which is ideal for separating areas for outlining, adding detail, texturing, and undercutting.

Gouges are able to scoop out wood that is ideal for creating curves and hollows in carvings.

Purchasing Woodcarving Supplies

In general, you will have better luck finding high quality knives, wood, and other supplies from shops that specialize in woodcarving than you will at most big box retailers, hardware stores, or hobby shops. If you don't have any local woodcarving or woodworking shops, there are several reputable online shops with a good selection of everything you may need. A good place to find these shops is in the advertising pages of *Woodcarving Illustrated* magazine. You can also ask for advice in online woodcarving forums, social media communities, or a local woodcarving club.

depth, and a #9 gouge is deep. The #11 gouge is the deepest, making a complete U shape and is sometimes referred to as a U-gouge or a veiner. The projects in this book can generally be completed without the use of gouges, although the Goldfish project will make use of a small U-gouge to add texture.

Saws

The projects in this book intentionally use only small, easy-to-find wood dimensions, 1" x 1" (2.5 x 2.5cm) or ¾" x ¾" (1.9 x 1.9cm), of varying lengths. If necessary, you can use a simple handsaw to cut longer pieces of wood to the lengths required to complete these projects. Many carvers add a scroll saw or band saw to their shop to help with cutting shapes from boards or to rough out larger pieces, but this is not necessary for beginners or long-term enjoyment of the hobby.

Other Helpful Items

- A pencil for drawing pattern and reference lines onto your wood
- A small ruler for measuring and marking your projects
- A brush (I use a toothbrush) for cleaning out rough areas
- A few bandages for unexpected nicks or cuts

Should I Sand My Carvings?

Whether to sand your carvings is a matter of personal preference. Sandpaper can be used either as a stylistic choice or to clean up messy and difficult-to-carve areas. When using sandpaper, it's a good idea to start with a higher grit, in the range of 200 to 300, and only move on to lower grits, if needed, keeping in mind that the lower the grit count, the rougher the sandpaper. You will also want to look for a flexible sandpaper, such as emery cloth. Personally, I prefer to see the knife and tool marks on the surface of my finished carvings, so I rarely sand my carvings. When it comes to cleaning up messy areas, I find that using a knife instead of sandpaper helps develop knife skills and leads to making cleaner cuts.

Sharpening

Knife sharpening is an essential skill for any whittler or woodcarver. For many beginners, the idea of sharpening the shiny new blade you just bought can be a little scary, but it doesn't need to be. Learning the basics of sharpening is easier than you might think, and I've found it to be an incredibly rewarding and empowering part of this hobby.

How to Tell if Your Blade Is Sharp: The Wood Test

Before learning to sharpen, you need to learn how to tell if your knife is sharp. Otherwise, you will have no way of knowing when to sharpen or if you have been successful at sharpening. There are many ways to test the sharpness of a knife, but the best way is by testing it on a piece of wood. By doing so, you will develop a feel for when your blade is starting to dull and it's time to strop or sharpen.

To test the sharpness of your blade, cut a corner off a block of wood at a steep angle, or cut straight across the grain on the end of a piece of wood. A sharp knife will leave a

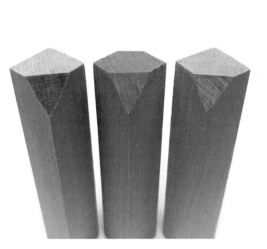

The knife in this photo should be pushed toward the far end of the strop, in the direction away from the cutting edge.

The cut on the left was made by a sharp blade, the cut in the middle was made with a blade that is slightly dull, and the cut on the right by a very dull blade.

completely flat surface that is shiny and slippery to the touch. A knife that is just starting to dull will leave a surface that is less shiny and a little cloudy. The cloudiness appears because your knife is starting to break the grain of the wood instead of cutting cleanly through it. This is a sign that it's time to strop your knife (see below). As a knife continues to dull, it will leave a cloudier surface, and it may also be more difficult to push through the wood. A knife that leaves distinct scratches and lines in the wood is very dull or damaged and is in need of sharpening.

Strops and compound come in a variety of sizes and colors.

How to Keep Your Knife Sharp: Stropping

Stropping is usually the final overall stage in knife sharpening in which a very fine cutting edge is added to a blade that is already sharp. However, it's easier to keep a knife sharp than to sharpen a dull knife, so the first skill you will want to learn is how to strop. A quality whittling knife can be kept sharp for years with just regular stropping.

Rub the stick of compound directly onto the strop to coat the leather with compound.

- **Strops and compound.** A strop is typically a piece of wood with a thin piece of leather glued rough side up on the wood. Stropping compound (also called honing, or polishing compound) usually comes in wax-like sticks or blocks. The stropping compound includes extremely fine grit abrasives that are held in place by the leather to accomplish the actual sharpening.
- **Applying compound.** If you are using a new strop for the first time, you will need to apply compound to the strop. Do this by rubbing the stick of compound onto the leather until there is a thin coat of compound covering the entire surface. It can be helpful to use a credit card to smooth and spread the compound evenly and avoid clumping.

Lay the blade on the near end of the stop with the cutting edge facing toward you, and then slide the blade away from you.

Turn the blade over and lay it on the far end of the strop with the cutting edge facing away from you, and then slide the blade toward you.

- **Stropping your knife.** Lay one side of the blade on the strop so that the surface leading to the cutting edge is completely flat. Next, gently slide the blade along the strop in the direction away from the cutting edge. Repeat this process 10 times, and then turn your blade over and complete the same number of strokes in the opposite direction. At the beginning and end of each stroke, take care to place the blade directly down or up from the strop without rolling the edge or allowing it to run off the end. You may use a finger to lightly hold the blade flat while you strop, but don't apply too much pressure to the blade. Continue until you have completed about 20 strokes on each side, then test the blade for sharpness and continue stropping, if needed.

The exact number of strokes and the frequency of stropping will vary based on your knife, the wood you are using, and the type of carving you are doing. In general, it's a good idea to stop and strop every 30 to 60 minutes while carving.

How to Sharpen Your Knife: The Sandpaper Method

If you find that your knife is still not sharp after stropping multiple times, then it's time to sharpen your knife. You can do this with sandpaper, which provides a cheap and easy alternative to sharpening stones.

MATERIALS

- Wet/dry sandpaper in approximately 800, 1,200, and 2,000 grits
- A completely flat surface, such as a thin piece of glass, plexiglass, or MDF that is 6" to 8" (15.2 x 20.3cm) long and at least a couple of inches wide
- A piece of plywood or other scrap wood with similar dimensions

■ **Assembling your materials.** Place the glass (or other flat surface) on top of your scrap wood base, and then place a piece of the wet/dry sandpaper directly on the glass so that the long edge of all three line up evenly. Smearing a few drops of water on the glass before setting the sandpaper on top works well as a temporary adhesive and avoids the mess of glue. Finally, smear a few drops of water on top of the sandpaper to act as a lubricant (this step is optional, but it can make the process a little smoother).

When sharpening a knife on wet/dry sandpaper, the knife should be pulled toward the right, away from the cutting edge.

A simple sharpening setup consisting of wet/dry sandpaper layered on top of a sheet of glass and a piece of scrap wood.

■ **Sharpening.** Place the blade of your knife on the sandpaper and apply the same process as described for stropping. Unless your blade is damaged or extremely dull, start with the 1,200-grit paper until you have completed at least 20 strokes on each side of the blade, alternating sides every 10 strokes. Test your blade for sharpness. If it is sharp, then repeat the process with the 2,000-grit paper, strop your blade, and then you are done. If it is not sharp, then repeat the process with the 1,200-grit paper and test again. If you find that after repeated sharpening on the 1,200-grit paper your knife is still not sharp, then move down to the 800-grit paper and follow the same process, moving on through the 1,200- and 2,000-grit paper and then stropping.

The exact number of strokes required and the exact grit counts of the paper can vary. You can substitute grit counts that are close to those described above (e.g., 1,000 instead of 1,200). You can also choose to take as many steps as you would like as long as you progress from lower to higher grit counts (e.g., 1,000, then 2,000, then 3,000, and so on). For especially dull or damaged blades, you may need to go down to 600- or 400-grit. While this method should work well for most whittling knives, it is always a good idea to review any sharpening recommendations provided by the knife manufacturer.

Safety

A cut-resistant glove and a thumb guard help reduce the chances of injuries when carving.

Sheaths don't just protect your tools; they protect you from cuts while handling and moving your tools.

Ensuring that you have the right safety equipment and are practicing safe carving practices is important to avoid injuries and ensure happy whittling for years to come.

Safety Equipment

- **Gloves.** A carving glove is an essential piece of equipment. Most cut-resistant gloves are made with a weave that includes Kevlar or steel. Some gloves come with rubber dots to help with grip, while others are reinforced with a rubber coating or leather. Each of these options have tradeoffs between protection, dexterity, and fit. Note that most gloves are cut resistant—not puncture proof. Wearing a glove is not a substitute for safe carving practices.
- **Thumb guards.** Generally, the glove is worn on your non-dominant hand, which is holding the wood you are carving. Thumb guards are used on your dominant hand in order to protect your thumb from certain cuts while holding your knife.

- **Sheaths.** Sheaths are just as helpful for protecting you as they are for protecting your knife. Sheath materials can range from leather and hard plastic to foam or other DIY options. If your knife didn't come with a sheath, a thick piece of foam, a bottle cork, or rubber tubing are all easy, cheap options for protecting your blade. Regardless of what you use, make sure you have a safe way to cover your blades when you aren't actively using them.

When rolled up, the blades of each knife and tool are well protected and safe to transport or store.

- **Tool storage.** In addition to blade covers, you will want to make sure all of your tools are properly protected when stored away. Tool rolls are an easy option for safe storage. They should be made of a thick, sturdy material, such as denim, canvas, or leather. They include individual slots for tools or knives and can be rolled and tied together for simple storage when not in use. Another option is a tool caddy, which will usually have circular slots, often lined with PVC tubes, in which tools can be stored handle up in order to provide easy access while protecting the cutting edge. Toolboxes and bags can be used as well, but make sure each tool has a separate cover or compartment so they are protected.

Safe Practices

Protective equipment is helpful, but the best way to avoid injury is by practicing safe carving habits. Here are a few tips to stay safe while carving.

- Whenever possible, carve away from yourself.
- If you must make a cut toward yourself, orient your knife and hand so that your fingers are not in the direct path of the knife.
- Always pay attention to where the knife would go if it continued in the direction you are pushing it.
- If you find that you are pushing hard, stop and try a smaller cut or different approach. Forcing a difficult cut often leads to injury.
- Never use parts of your body (e.g. your leg) to brace a piece of wood in place while carving it.

The Basic Cuts of Whittling

Push cuts provide you with more control over your knife, as you hold the knife with your dominant hand and use the thumb of your non-dominant hand to push the blade.

Push cut. Perform the basic push cut by holding your knife in your dominant hand and your wood in your non-dominant hand. Place the thumb of your non-dominant hand on the spine of the knife blade, and use it to push the blade through the wood. In this way, your dominant hand provides control and counterbalance while your non-dominant hand pushes the knife. This two-handed approach may feel a little awkward at first, but it provides excellent control and will feel natural with a little practice.

Make sure to anchor your thumb on the bottom or side of your carving for leverage and control while using paring cuts.

Paring cut. A paring cut, also called a pull cut, is used in situations where it is not possible or practical to make a push cut. The cut is performed with just your dominant hand, while your wood is held with your non-dominant hand. To safely make a paring cut, hold the knife with the cutting edge oriented toward you. Anchor your thumb on the bottom or side of your carving to provide leverage and control, being careful to keep it out of the direct path of the blade. Then, gently pull the knife toward you, through the wood.

an angle, then turn the wood around and make another push cut from the other direction so that they meet in the middle, leaving a V-shaped notch in the wood. To ensure your two cuts meet at the right location, it can sometimes be helpful to start by placing a stop cut at the center of your V-cut.

Carvers create basic shapes and separate parts of their carvings by using a combination of stop and push cuts.

Stop cut. A stop cut is made by pushing the cutting edge of the blade straight into the wood. Position the blade with your dominant hand, and then use the thumb of your non-dominant hand to push the blade directly into the wood. This cut is used to create a stopping point for another cut, usually a push cut. The combination of stop cut/ push cut is the primary method for separating different parts of your carving and creating basic shapes.

Chip cuts consist of three small cuts that make up a triangle to create details.

Chip cut. The chip cut, sometimes referred to as a triangle cut, is made up of three small cuts in the shape of a triangle. Start by inserting the tip of the knife into the wood along one side of the triangle, with the tip going in right at the tip of the triangle. Perform a similar cut on the second side of the triangle, meeting at the point of your first cut. Then, make a final, horizontal cut from one side of the triangle to the other to remove a small triangle chip from the wood. If the chip doesn't come out on your first try, repeat the cuts until it does—never use your knife to pry wood out.

V-cuts are used to distinguish two areas on a carving and can be used to create facial features and add details.

V-cut. A V-cut, or V-shaped cut, is two cuts that meet in the center to create a V shape. To complete a V-cut, make one push cut into the wood at

Painting and Finishing

Painting

Painting is one of the many ways you can finish your piece once you have finished carving.

Small bottles of acrylic paints, such as these, come in a variety of brands and colors and should last a long time.

Painting and finishing are all about presenting your final work in the best possible way. A splash of color or a finish that brings out the natural beauty of the wood can add a lot of interest and character to your final piece. For many beginners, the idea of painting or adding a finish to your carvings can be scary. I painted almost none of my carvings for my first year, mostly out of fear that I would ruin the pieces that I was so proud of carving. In this section, I will share some simple, beginner-friendly methods to paint and finish your carvings. No matter how you finish your carvings, it's important to remember that you are working with a piece of wood. The colors, paints, and finishes should serve to highlight the shape of your carving and the natural beauty of the wood, never to cover it up. First, let's take a look at the equipment and materials that you will need to paint and finish your carvings.

Acrylic paint is the most common type of paint used for carvings and is recommended for beginners. The great thing about acrylic paints is that they are easy to find and relatively cheap. Because it is generally recommended to water down acrylic paints (see page 22), even small bottles will last for a long time. Buy an assortment of colors and brands, and try them out to see what you like. You can always substitute the specific shades and colors used in a particular project for what you have, and you can also mix your paints to lighten, darken, or create new colors.

The types of brushes you use depends on what you are painting on your carving.

Flat brushes, such as these, can be used for painting large, mostly flat surfaces.

Round brushes are useful for painting open areas of carvings and getting paint into cracks and crevices.

Small detail brushes are useful for painting fine details or borders between colors.

Brushes

Brushes come in many shapes and sizes. The size and shape of brushes used to paint your carvings will depend on what you are painting but is also a matter of personal preference. There are three general types of brushes that I recommend for getting started.

- **Flat brushes.** Flat brushes are helpful for painting large, mostly flat surfaces. Their straight edge can be useful for painting along borders. The edge of the brush could be completely straight or skewed. The skewed flat brush can be helpful for getting into difficult corners or painting details.
- **Round brushes.** Round brushes can be used for painting any open areas but are especially helpful in areas that are too small to comfortably fit a flat brush. They are also good for painting areas that have a lot of texture as the pointed tip is generally easier to get into cracks and crevices. These brushes come in various widths and lengths, with some being more suited for filling areas and others more helpful for painting lines and details.
- **Fine-detail brushes.** Fine-detail brushes are very small, round brushes. These are helpful for painting small details on your carvings or painting precise borders in areas where two colors are coming together.

Other Equipment

In addition to paints and brushes, there are a variety of other tools that can be helpful to have available when painting.

- **Palette.** Use a palette for holding your paints and mixing them with one another or water. I use a simple white plastic palette. Some carvers like to use a glass surface for mixing paints; you can even use a paper plate.
- **Pencil.** Keep a pencil handy to make reference marks and draw on any detailed features prior to painting.

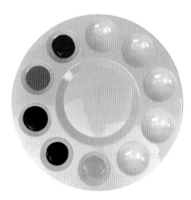

A paint palette is helpful for holding, mixing, and watering down paints while painting your carvings.

- **Toothpicks.** Toothpicks can be dipped in paint, and then used to draw lines with paint, like pens.
- **Embossing tools.** Embossing tools are small round metal balls at the end of a stick. They are great for dipping in paint and then pressing onto your carving to paint dots. They are optional, as you can achieve similar results with the rounded end of a paintbrush handle, pencil, or toothpick.
- **Cup of water.** You will want to keep a cup of water handy while painting to both clean your brushes and water down your paints.
- **Eyedropper.** This is optional, but many carvers prefer to use an eyedropper to add drops of water to their paints.
- **Paper towels.** For cleaning up messes, mainly. Paper towels are also used in many finishing techniques.
- **Carving knife.** Used to clean up any rough areas on the carving that you find while painting or to remove painting mistakes.

Embossing tools, such as these, provide a simple option for painting dots of various sizes onto your carvings.

Holding Your Carving While Painting

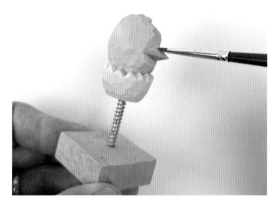

To avoid paint smudges while painting, I recommend you make a simple holder so you do not have to hold your carving.

Holding your carving while painting can be a challenge. To avoid unwanted paint smudges from fingers that get in the way, you can make a simple holder. There are a variety of ways to do this, but most options involve a small screw that can be screwed into the carving and is attached to another piece of wood that is easier to hold.

The basic holder that I use for painting is a wood screw that is screwed through a flat square piece of ½" (1.3cm) wood. The tip of the screw can be gently screwed by hand into the bottom of the carving that is being painted, then the wood provides a handhold. It also doubles as a stand for carvings while they dry between layers of paint or finish.

Water Down Your Paints

Full-strength acrylic paint is very thick and can be difficult to apply evenly. Even if you do get an even application of full-strength paint, it will completely hide your wood and leave a thick, plastic-looking appearance on the final carving. Watered-down paints are easier to apply evenly and allow the wood grain to show through, making it clear that it's a carved piece of wood.

To water down your paints, add a small amount of paint to your palette, and then add drops of water to your desired amount. You can use an eyedropper, or just dip your finger in a cup of water and drop it in. Stir the paint and water with a toothpick, paintbrush handle, or embossing tool. Once the paint and water are mixed to a consistent thickness, you are ready to paint.

Add a few drops of water to a few drops of paint in your palette, and stir them together to water your down your paints prior to painting.

The amount of water you add to the paint is largely a matter of personal preference. Many carvers prefer very diluted paints and will create a wash with as much as 90% water and 10% paint. In general, I prefer my colors to be a little stronger and mostly use a 50/50 paint-water mix. To keep things simple in

this book, I will refer to slightly watered-down (25% water, 75% paint), watered-down (50% water, 50% paint) and heavily watered-down (75% water, 25% paint) mixes. All of these are rough estimates, and you can experiment to find what works for you. In general, starting with paint that is more watered down is desirable as you can always add more layers of paint, if needed.

How to Paint

When it comes to painting, follow a simple process of using brushes to apply paint to your carvings. Experience is the greatest teacher, so don't hesitate to get started and find what works for you. Here are some tips to help you get the best results.

- Start with lighter colors and progress toward darker colors. If you are sloppy or make mistakes with light colors, it will be easier to cover them up with darker colors.
- When painting along borders between colors, paint the border area first with a small detail brush, and then use a larger brush to paint the whole area. It can also be helpful to use less watered-down paint directly along the border to avoid bleeding between colors.
- The end grain of a carving—at the top or bottom of your carving if the grain is running vertically—will suck in more paint than the sides. Plan on multiple coats in these areas.

A flat brush can be used to paint various parts of a carvings, such as the body of a whittled person, a shell, and beard of an old man.

 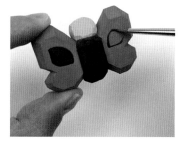 

A fine-detail brush can paint thinner and hard to reach places on carvings, such as between the shell on a hatching chick, the outline of a section of a butterfly wing, and the eyebrows on a face.

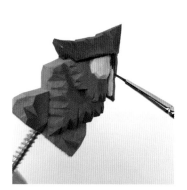  

A fine-detail brush can also be used to paint borders, such as the border between the hat and hair on the gnome and the border of the hair around a face.

Keeping a steady hand while painting details can be tricky. While painting the eye on this chick, I am bracing my left hand against the table and one finger of my right hand against the carving to avoid any mistakes that could be made due to a shaky hand.

Painting the hair on the top of the head of this whittle person will require more paint than other areas, as the paint will absorb much more quickly through the end grain on the top of the carving.

A toothpick dipped in paint can be used to paint on details, such as the smile on this whittle person.

- When painting fine details, anchor one of your fingers onto the carving or brace your hands against the table to keep your hands steady.

Using Your Knife as an Eraser

A knife is used to shave off unwanted paint from the head of this whittle person carving.

If you make a mistake when painting, don't panic! Your knife can almost always be used to erase mistakes. If you get paint on an area of your carving that you didn't mean to, gently use your knife to shave off the undesirable paint. You can use your knife to clean up borders between colors, or even to remove complete features and repaint them if you aren't happy with the results.

Painting Eyes

Adding eyes to your carvings can bring them to life and add a lot of character. There are a lot of ways to paint eyes, ranging from simple dots to detailed blends of colors and highlights. Below, I'm going to share two simple options for eye painting. Always draw the eyes on with a pencil to ensure you have the positioning correct first. You may also want to practice on a scrap piece of wood or paper. If you make a mistake, don't worry! You can use your knife to shave the eye off and try again.

Happy Eyes

These eyes convey a cute and happy demeaner that is effective for a wide variety of carvings. To paint the happy eyes, dip a toothpick in undiluted black paint and draw the eyes on. It may take a couple tries to get the thickness just right. Practice first and experiment to figure out how much paint is needed on the toothpick and what angle to hold it to get your desired line thickness. It is also possible to do this with a fine-tip brush, but I find it easier to get consistent results with the toothpick. For a twist on the basic happy eye, try adding a couple eyelashes coming up on the outside edge of each eye.

A toothpick is used to paint a happy eye onto a chick.

An embossing tool is first used to paint a large black dot for an eye on a whittle person.

Next, an embossing tool is used to paint a small white dot on the eye of a whittle person.

Dot Eyes

Dot eyes are made with a large color dot and a small white dot inside (see page 25). Start by dipping an embossing tool into undiluted black paint, and then touch the end of the tool directly onto the wood where you want to place the eye. If you don't have an embossing tool, the rounded end of a paintbrush handle or any other object that comes to a small, round tip can be used. Practice first to ensure you know how much paint you need to make an eye of your desired size. Wait until the black part of the eye has completely dried, and then use a smaller embossing tool or toothpick tip to add a white dot inside each eye. In general, you want the white dots to be in the same relative position of each eye (e.g., both in the top right) and not in the center. Feel free to experiment with different colors, dot sizes, and numbers of dots to make the eyes your own.

Antiquing and Dry-Brushing

When painting a large area of a carving a single color, it can obscure the details of your carving, making it difficult to see the actual cuts and textures you have made. Antiquing and dry-brushing are two common techniques used to create contrast between high and low surfaces, making your cuts more recognizable. Although they accomplish similar results, they do so in different ways. Antiquing creates contrast by darkening the deeper portions of a carving, while dry-brushing does so by highlighting the higher parts. Both antiquing and dry-brushing take place after initial painting and before adding any final finishes to the carving.

Antiquing

Antiquing is a process of "aging" your carving—it makes your carving look older by darkening the deeper areas of your carving while simultaneously adding a worn look to the higher, smoother surfaces.

The beards on the gnomes in this picture were painted with the same shade of gray. The gnome on the left was antiqued, darkening the deeper areas of the beard, while the beard on the right was dry-brushed highlighting the higher facets of the beard.

The wood spirits in this picture were both painted the same color. The effects of antiquing can be seen in the wood spirit on the right.

Antiquing solutions can be easily found in craft stores.

You will want to make sure the paint on your carving is thoroughly dry before antiquing. You can buy ready-to-use solutions or mix them yourself. In general, premade antiquing solutions come in various shades and have the consistency of sticky brown paint. For beginners, I recommend starting with premade antiquing solutions, such as Antiquing Medium by FolkArt/Plaid or Gel Stains by Americana/DecoArt. Follow these steps to antique your carvings.

3 **Immediately use a paper towel or soft cloth to gently wipe excess antiquing solution off of the carving.** This will leave solution in the deeper crevices and cuts while leaving a smooth but worn look on the higher parts of the carving. Be careful not to rub too hard, or you could rub off paint or remove the antiquing solution from the crevices where you want it to stay. Allow the carving to dry. After it is dried you can finish with any other finishing product that you would like.

1 **Water down your antiquing solution.** Just like paints, antiquing solution at full strength can give you a much stronger appearance than desired. I would recommend starting with about a $^{50}/_{50}$ water–antiquing solution mixture and adjust from there.

2 **Paint the antiquing solution over your carving with a large round brush.**

Tips for Antiquing

- Antiquing over bright-colored paints will severely darken the colors and can sometimes result in a look that comes across as dirty instead of aged. For this situation, start with a heavily watered-down solution.
- You can antique just specific areas of a carving, such as a beard or hair. Just be careful when rubbing the solution off not to smear it onto other areas of the carving, as it can be difficult to remove.
- An option that provides a more subtle antiqued look is to paint the solution only into the specific cracks and crevices of the carving that you want to darken, instead of the whole surface.

Dry-Brushing

Dry-brushing is a painting technique that involves lightly painting the high points of your carving to highlight the facets. It works by briskly brushing with a dry-brush that has been loaded with a very small amount of paint. The paint sticks to the higher portions of the carving without getting into the cracks. Use a round brush with some fluff to it (avoid flat brushers or liner brushes) and use full-strength paint. Dry-brushing is most commonly done with a shade of white paint, but you can experiment with other colors. Here's how to dry-brush.

1 Load your brush with paint. Dip your dry paintbrush into full-strength white paint, and then rub it back and forth in every direction on a paper towel until you appear to have brushed most of the paint off the brush. Repeat this process four to five times. If the bristles of the brush start to matte together, press them into the paper towel to separate the bristles.

2 Using a brisk sweeping motion, brush your loaded brush back and forth over the desired area.

Tips for Dry-Brushing

- The action of dry-brushing is quite easy, but getting just the right amount of paint on the brush can take practice. It is a good idea to create some practice pieces to experiment on.
- Just like painting, you can lightly dry-brush or heavily dry-brush. You may prefer one look or the other, but in general, you want to start very lightly. You can always add more, but it is difficult to remove paint that has been dry-brushed onto a carving.
- While you can dry-brush any carved surface, dry-brushing works especially well on heavily textured areas.

Finishing

After painting your carving, it is a good idea to add a finish to seal the wood, protect the paint, and preserve the carving. I'm going to focus on just a few simple options that should work well for beginners with little to no experience with wood finishes.

Howard Feed-N-Wax

Howard Feed-N-Wax is a mixture of orange oil and beeswax that both seals and adds a nice finish that highlights grain and enhances the colors of

Howard Feed-N-Wax is recommended for beginners, as it is easy and safe to use.

the wood/paint. It is a recommended option for beginners because it is easy to use, gives good consistent results, and has none of the dangers that come with some other finishes. You can finish painted or unpainted wooden surfaces with Howard Feed-N-Wax, but be aware that you will not be able to paint over or add any other finish once you are done. Here's how to apply it.

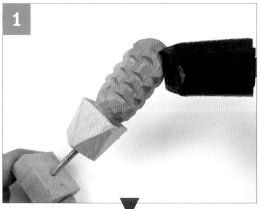

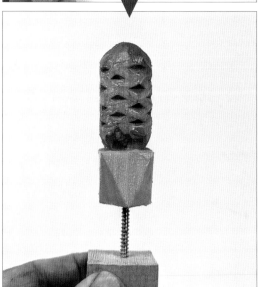

2 **Wipe off the excess finish with a paper towel or soft rag.** Let your carving sit for at least eight hours.

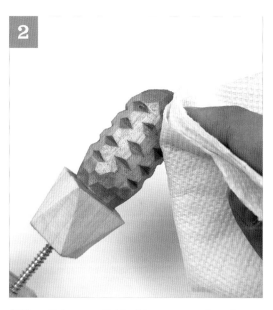

1 **Completely coat your carving with Howard Feed-N-Wax.** Be sure to get it into all the nooks and crannies of your carving. I use a square sponge brush, but any paintbrush or even a cloth will do. Let your carving sit, fully coated, for 5 to 10 minutes.

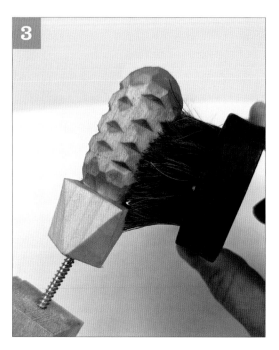

3 **Buff it with a soft brush, such as a shoe brush.** Let your carving sit for another eight hours and buff again.

Other Finishes

All of the carvings in this book are finished with Howard Feed-N-Wax, but there are other options that you may want to consider. Below, I will share a few of the more common finishes that are worth considering if you are a beginner. Always be sure to read and follow the manufacturer's instructions for applying finishes.

Spray sealants are a good option for finishing carvings, as it adds an extra gloss to your finished piece.

Boiled linseed oil is often used to bring the grain out on lighter woods.

Online Carving Communities and Social Media Groups

Social media groups and discussion forums can be a great source of inspiration, encouragement, and community-building for beginning carvers. Here are a few tips for engaging in online communities.

- **Get inspired.** Seeing others' work can provide inspiration and ideas for your own carvings. If you attempt a carving design or technique that you picked up from someone on social media, be sure to give them credit when you post your version of their work.
- **Share your own work.** Sharing your own work can be helpful for getting feedback and for creating your own library of progress. Remember that we all learn and progress at different rates, so avoid the trap of comparing your work to others and focus just on comparing your work to your own previous work.
- **Interact with fellow carvers.** Don't be afraid to ask questions. The carving community tends to be extremely supportive and encouraging. You will likely get good answers to your questions, although you may get a variety of responses.

- **Spray sealants.** Sealants that come in an aerosol spray for sealing paintings are also a good option for finishing carvings. Many carvers prefer a matte finish spray because it seals without adding a lot of extra gloss, leaving a more natural appearance to your carving. Spray sealants can easily be found in the paint section of most hobby stores.
- **Wax finishes.** Wax finishes are easy to apply and provide a nice coating of protection for carvings. The general process is similar to that described for Howard Feed-N-Wax. Paste wax or beeswax work well.

Should I Treat the Wood Prior to Painting?

All of the projects in this book are finished by painting directly onto the wood with no pretreatment. This is the simplest option for beginners, but there are options available for pre-treating wood. Adding oil to carvings prior to painting has become a common practice for many carvers. This can keep paints from bleeding too much and can help the wood grain show through the paints more clearly. Other options include coating the whole piece in a very heavily watered-down wash of paint or using a pretreatment product, such as Gesso. These options can sometimes help apply paint more evenly. Ultimately, treating wood prior to painting is a matter of preference. Try it, and see if you are happy with results.

- **Oil finishes**. Oil finishes are another popular option because they are easy to apply to three-dimensional objects and provide a nice, natural finish while sealing and protecting the wood. Boiled linseed oil is very popular because of its ability to bring out the grain in lightly colored woods, including basswood. However, it has a strong odor and the added danger of potential spontaneous combustion from oil-soaked rags. If you choose to try an oil finish, be sure to closely follow the manufacturer's recommendations for applying the oil and cleaning up any oil-soaked rags.

Adding Accessories

After painting and finishing, it's time to consider how to display your finished work. Often this involves simply finding a shelf or desk on which to set the carving for display, but some carvings lend themselves to serving a more useful or more personal purpose. It's common to find carvings that have been turned into ornaments, magnets, zipper pulls, bottle stoppers, necklaces, earrings, and more. In this section, I'll provide two easy options for mounting/displaying your carvings.

Eyelets

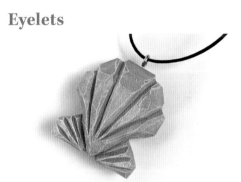

An eyelet and a leather cord can also be added to turn a shell carving into a necklace.

Eyelets are added to carvings in order to hang them or attach them to other objects. You can use the eyelet to attach a string to create an ornament, a necklace or pendant, a keychain, or a zipper pull. Eyelets can be purchased at most hobby shops in various sizes and colors. You can attach an eyelet by simply pushing the threaded tip into the desired location on your carving and turning it by hand to screw it into the wood.

  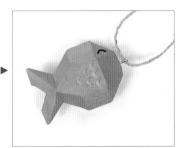

An eyelet and string are added to a fish carving to turn it into an ornament.

Magnets

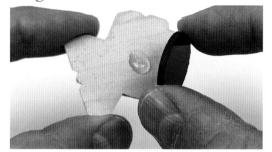

A magnet is applied to the back of a carving using superglue and adhesive backing.

Magnets are another great option for carvings. You can buy magnets at a hobby shop or online. In general, look for a thin, flat magnet. Although many magnets come with adhesive backing, it is a good idea to add a few drops of superglue before applying the magnet to the carving in order to ensure that it stays on. If you're applying the magnet to an area that has been painted, first sand or shave

the paint off, then glue the magnet on. If desired, you can also drill or carve a recess into your carving when placing the magnet so that the back of the wood lies flush with the surface it is attached to. If you decide to mount a carving on a magnet, you may want to further flatten the back of the carving before doing so. These shells were carved on a split piece of wood so that the back would be flat.

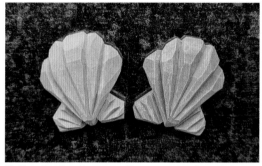

Shell carvings have been turned into magnets and attached to a sheet of metal.

Flattening

Many of the projects in this book use a technique I call "flattening" prior to drawing the pattern onto the wood.

   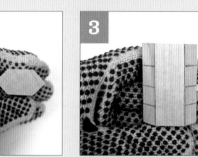

1. Use a pencil to draw a horizontal centerline on each face of the wood. Then, use your knife to remove one of the corners of the block, lowering that corner until the area between the center lines on each side of the corner is completely flat.

2. Repeat on the corner on the opposite side of block. When your block is completely flattened, it will look like the images above.

3. Now you are ready to draw on the pattern. I find it easiest to draw horizontal reference lines at ½" (1.3cm) intervals on the outside edges of the front and back of the wood. These create grids that make it simple to draw the remaining pattern lines on either freehand, or with a ruler as a guide.

Note: This technique is used in the first step of the Goldfish, Seashell, Grumpy/Happy Cat, Super Simple Gnome, Butterfly, Pineapple, and Rose in Vase projects.

PROJECTS

Whittle People

Whittling a sphere on the end of stick of wood is a common task for beginners. It helps develop basic skills related to shaping and symmetry that can be applied to shaping a wide variety of carvings. This project is designed to take that simple beginner's task and turn it into a finished piece. If you're going to carve a sphere for practice, you might as well make something fun out of it! If you are new to carving, this is a good place to start. If you are experienced, or are just looking for more of a challenge, start with the basic design and add your own details or elements to the design.

Pattern

Photocopy at 100%.

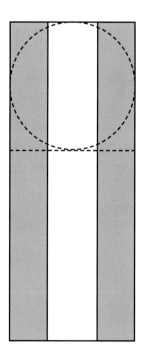

MATERIALS

- Basswood, 1" x 1" x 2 ½" (2.5 x 2.5 x 6.4cm)
- FolkArt by Plaid acrylic paints: Uniform Blue, Real Brown, Pure Black, Vintage White
- Howard Feed-N-Wax

TOOLS

- Carving knife
- Ruler
- Flat paintbrush
- Round paintbrush
- Pencil

1 **Use a pencil to draw the basic pattern lines onto the carving.** The solid lines and shaded areas should be drawn on each side. The dotted lines will be drawn on later, when needed.

2 Remove the outside corners. Use push cuts along each outside corner of the wood block to remove the shaded areas in the pattern. Start by cutting along the middle of one edge and carving up toward the end, using multiple cuts to flatten the corner down to the pattern lines. Then, turn the wood around and remove the wood from the same corner in the other direction, until the corner has been completely flattened. Follow the same process to remove all four corners, until the shape of the block as viewed from the top is an octagon.

3 Round the block to a cylinder. Use push cuts to gently remove the eight hard corners remaining around the outside of the wood. Continue removing hard corners, until you have shaped the wood into a cylinder. When viewed from the top or bottom, the wood should look like a circle.

4 Define the bottom of the head. Use your pencil to draw a horizontal pattern line 1" (2.5cm) down from the top of the wood. Make a series of stop cuts directly along this line all the way around your carving. Draw another horizontal line with your pencil about ⅓" (8.5mm) above the previous line. Then, holding the carving with the head pointed down, make a push cut started from the new line you just drew into the stop cut at the bottom of the head. Using the new line as a reference point, make a row of roughly even push cuts all around the head, starting at the reference line and ended at the base of the head. You will likely want to complete each of these cuts twice in order to make them deep enough.

5 Finish the bottom of the head. Make another row of push cuts into the stop cut at the base of the head, this time starting about halfway between where you started your previous row of cuts and the base of the head. If possible, start each cut on an edge between facets created in the previous step. You will need to repeat the stop cut to deepen it as you go along and will likely want to make each cut twice to go deep enough. After completing this, repeat the process one more time, again starting about halfway between your previous row of cuts and the bottom of the head.

6 Start the top of the head. Draw another horizontal line with your pencil ⅓" (8.5mm) down from the top of the head. Holding the wood with the head pointed up, make a row of push cuts starting at this reference line and going up to the top of the wood. Make each cut twice, in order to make them deep enough. Focus on making slightly overlapping cuts at regular intervals and equal depths.

7 Finish the top of the head. Starting about halfway between where you started your previous row of cuts and the top of the head, make another row of push cuts toward the top of the head. Make these a little deeper, as you will need to completely round off the top of the head. If possible, start each cut at an edge where two facets from your previous step meet. Follow this with another row of push cuts, again about halfway between your previous row and the top of the head. If necessary, make a final series of cuts directly across the top of the grain to completely round off the top. Leave no flat, uncarved wood on the top of the carving.

Should I Practice by Carving the Same Design Multiple Times or by Carving Something New?

When learning to whittle, there is great benefit in carving the same thing multiple times. It gives you a chance to learn from your mistakes, experiment with different techniques to accomplish the same task, and provides a very tangible way to gauge your progress. At the same time, there is great benefit in carving different things. It challenges you to learn new skills, it gives you the chance to apply existing skills in new situations, and it can be motivating to try something new. As you continue to carve, you may find that you prefer to always be trying something new, or to keep doing the same thing over and over. Consider challenging yourself from time to time to learn by either repeating a process several times or pushing yourself to try new things. In my case, I generally prefer to try new designs. However, I've been surprised at how much I've learned by carving the same thing multiple times and finding new and subtle ways to improve my work.

8 Check for symmetry and adjust, if needed. Take a moment to inspect the overall roundness of the head. If you are just learning to whittle, it's likely that you will find some areas that are uneven. I usually end up smoothing the area right along the reference lines drawn in steps 4 and 6. Make additional cuts, if necessary, to finish rounding the head, but remember that it doesn't have to be perfect, and leaving the facets—the flat surfaces made by your knife in the wood—can be a desirable aesthetic for your finished work.

9 Smooth the shoulders. Round off the hard corner created at the top of the shoulders by using the tip of your knife and cutting along the edge. Pay attention to the location of the tip so that you don't accidentally scratch the bottom of the head during this process.

10 Paint the body and hair. Use a flat brush with watered-down (50% water, 50% paint) acrylic paint in the color of your choice to paint the body. Use a round brush with slightly watered-down (25% water, 75% paint) paint for the hair, painting the color and style of your choice. You may want to use a pencil to lightly draw in the area of the hair before painting.

From Square to Circle

Consider the cross section of your piece of wood as essentially a square. If you remove the corners of the square, you will end up with an octagon. If you do this again by removing the eight corners of the octagon, you will technically end up with a hexadecagon, but this is close enough to a circle that no one will notice (although you should definitely brag to your friends about your ability to whittle a hexadecagon). This same basic technique can be applied in a variety of contexts, such as carving round noses, balls, hats, and more.

If you need to carve a circle, start by drawing a square and remove corners until you have a circle.

The progression of rounding a square to a circular shape is shown from left to right.

11 Paint the face. Draw on the location of the eyes and smile with a pencil. Then, use a toothpick dipped in black or red paint to paint on the smile. Paint on your desired eyes as described on page 25. Leave the rest of the face unpainted. Finish with a coat of Howard Feed-N-Wax.

How to Deal with Breaking Wood

As you begin to carve, it won't take long before you experience breaking wood. Most likely, you will be whittling along the side of a piece of wood, right along the grain, and a piece will break off, leaving ugly jagged streaks along your wood. When this happens, don't worry. Even with good wood, you will sometimes find sections where the grain isn't perfectly straight, and there is a simple solution to this problem. When you encounter an area of breaking wood, simply turn the wood around and carve in the opposite direction. Over time, you will start to get a feel for when this is happening. Your knife will feel like it is getting pulled into the wood instead of smoothly running through. If you start to feel this, you can avoid breakages by stopping mid-cut and turning the wood around to carve in the opposite direction.

The areas on the sides of this wood have carved off smoothly, but the wood in the center has broken off, leaving large, jagged edges of varying depth.

Simple Cactus

This little potted cactus is a fun and simple project that looks great on a shelf or desk. Aside from looking great, it's also a perfect project for beginners. While carving this cactus, you will learn to carve large, flat surfaces and get plenty of practice making V-cuts. Once you have the basic pattern down, try adjusting the design to make your own variations on the shapes for the base and the cactus. You'll soon be able to enjoy your own small wooden garden without the danger of getting poked or the hassle of keeping them watered!

MATERIALS

- Basswood, 1" x 1" x 3" (2.5 x 2.5 x 7.6cm)
- FolkArt by Plaid acrylic paint: Fresh Cut Grass
- Howard Feed-N-Wax

TOOLS

- Carving knife
- Flat paintbrush
- Pencil/pen
- Ruler

Pattern

Photocopy at 100%.

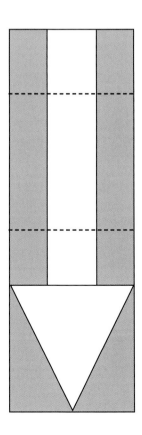

1 Apply the pattern. Use a pencil and ruler to draw the pattern onto each side of the wood block.

2 Separate the base. Remove the shaded corners on each side of the cactus. Begin by holding the wood with the base of the cactus pointing up and placing a stop cut at one of the corners where the base meets the plant. Carve up to the stop cut from about a ½" (1.3cm) beneath it. Continue the cuts until you have carved down to the depth indicated by the pattern lines. Repeat on the other corners.

3 Flatten the sides. Turn your wood around so you are carving toward the top of the cactus, and use push cuts to remove the rest of the shaded area from the corners on each side. Use multiple cuts and continue until you have completely flattened each corner. When you are done, the wood should look like an octagon from the top.

4 Taper the bottom of the cactus. Use your pencil to add a horizontal reference line ½" (1.3cm) above the base. Holding the wood with the base pointing up, draw a triangle from this reference line, starting at a corner and extending across the flat face on either side, up to the base as indicated in the image. Place a stop cut along the point where the cactus meets the base and then carve up to it, removing the shaded triangle area. Rotate your wood and repeat the process until you have made a similar cut along each hard corner around the outside of cactus.

5 Finish the bottom. Starting at a hard corner about ¼" (6.4mm) from the base, make another stop cut along the base and make a deep push cut, further tapering the cactus toward the bottom. Rotate and repeat all the way around the cactus. Repeat the process one more time, about ⅛" (3.2mm) up from the base.

6 Taper the top. Use your pencil to add a horizontal reference line ½" (1.3cm) below the top of the cactus. Holding the wood with the top of the cactus up, draw a triangle from this reference line, starting at one corner and extending across the flat face on either side, as indicated in the image. Use push cuts to remove the area indicated by the triangle. Rotate and repeat the process around the entire cactus.

7 Finish the top. Starting about ¼" (6.4mm) down from the top, find a hard corner and make a steep push cut, further flattening the top. Rotate the piece and repeat, making a similar cut at each hard corner all the way around the cactus. Then, starting about ⅛" (3.2mm) from the top, make steep cuts almost directly across the grain to round the top, until the top is completely rounded.

8 Carve the base. Holding the wood with the base pointing up, use multiple push cuts to remove the shaded triangles on each corner of the base. Try to leave each triangle area with a completely flat surface.

9 Add texture. Add horizontal V-cuts along each hard corner along the side of the cactus. Start at one corner and add a V-cut in the middle and another along each of the horizontal reference lines drawn in steps 4 and 6. Rotate the cactus, and on the next corner, add two V-cuts spaced evenly between the three you made on the first corner. Continue the process around the entire cactus.

Flat-Plane Carving

Flat-plane carving is distinctive for leaving large flat surfaces, or planes, on the outside of the carving. Flat-plane carving originated as a style of FolkArt in Scandinavia and has gone on to inspire and influence countless woodcarvers. Traditionally, flat-plane carvings are completed with just one knife, which is used to make clean, bold cuts, conveying complex shapes with an appealing simplicity.

Carving Flat Surfaces

The progression shown in these three images shows how to use a series of smaller cuts to create one final flat surface.

Flat, smooth surfaces can help clearly define the shape of a carving while also creating a distinct and visually appealing style. It may look like they are made with one large cut, but it is often the case that a flat surface on a carving is the result of a final cut after making several smaller cuts. The images here show a progression of cuts used to create the smooth surface in step 8. This technique of flattening surfaces will be used in many of the projects found later in this book. As a beginner, you should take your time and use as many cuts as you need in order to completely flatten these surfaces.

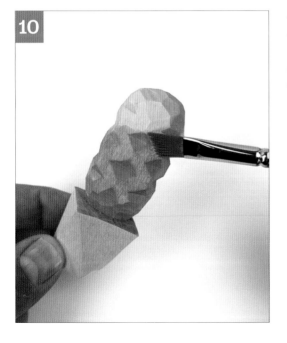

10 Paint and finish. Use a flat paintbrush to paint the body of the cactus with a heavily watered-down (75% water, 25% paint) light green. Add coats of watered-down paint until you reach your desired appearance. Leave the base unfinished. After the paint has completely dried, finish with a coat of Howard Feed-N-Wax.

Hatching Chicks

These happy little chicks are quick and fun to carve. They look good in a variety of colors and are conveniently sized for hiding in Easter eggs or adding to your spring decorations. More than just a cute project, these chicks are also great for building your skills as a beginning carver. They provide good opportunity for practicing rounding skills, as well as learning how to carve a sharp beak and adding fine details. After carving a few chicks, consider adding the optional nests for an extra element of fun.

MATERIALS

- Basswood, 1" x 1" x 1 ½" (2.5 x 2.5 x 3.8cm), for the chick
- Basswood, 1 ½" x 1 ½" x ¾" (3.8 x 3.8 x 1.9cm), for the nest
- FolkArt by Plaid acrylic paint: Vintage White, Pure Orange, Skyline, Pure Black, Real Brown
- Americana by DecoArt acrylic paint: Cadmium Yellow, Bubblegum Pink
- Howard Feed-N-Wax

TOOLS

- Carving knife
- V-tool, ⅜" (10mm) 90 degrees (optional, for nest)
- Drill with 1 ⅞" (48mm) Forstner bit (optional, for nest)
- Pencil
- Ruler
- Flat paintbrush
- Round paintbrush
- Detail paintbrush
- Toothpicks

Pattern

Photocopy at 100%.

FRONT

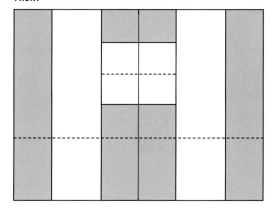

BACK

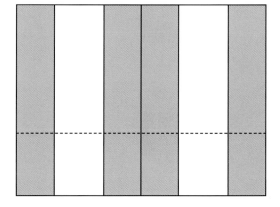

Carving Small Pieces of Wood

If you find that a project is too small to hold comfortably, you have a couple options. One is to carve it on the end of a longer stick of 1" x 1" (2.5 x 2.5cm) wood and then cut it off with a saw when you are done. This is a technique used by many carvers to create a kind of temporary handle to hold onto as they carve. Another option is to scale the carving up to a larger size. This project scales nicely to a 1 ½" x 1 ½" x 2 ¼" (3.8 x 3.8 x 5.7cm) piece of wood.

The chick on the left is carved on the end of 1" x 1" x 6" (2.5 x 2.5 x 15.2cm) piece of basswood. The chick on the right has been carved on a scaled-up piece of 1 ½" x 1 ½" x 2 ¼" (3.8 x 3.8 x 5.7cm) piece of basswood.

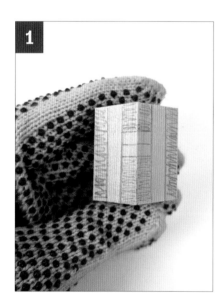

1 Apply the pattern. Use a pencil to draw the pattern lines onto the wood. The front pattern and back pattern each show two 1" x 1.5" (2.5 x 3.8cm) faces of the wood. The remaining pattern lines will be drawn on as you go along.

2 Rough out the chick. On the front of the carving, place a stop cut at the bottom of the beak area, and carve up to it from below, until the shaded area beneath the beak is completely flat. Follow a similar process to remove the wood above the beak. Then, use push cuts to carve off the remaining three hard corners indicated by the shared areas in the pattern. When viewed from the top or bottom, the wood should look like an octagon, with just the beak area sticking out on one corner.

3 Round the sides. Extend the stop cuts along the top and bottom of the beak area, and carve into these stop cuts to remove the hard corners running along each side of the beak. Smooth the remaining hard edges around the entire carving, until the carving has a cylindrical shape.

4 Round the bottom. Use the pencil to draw a horizontal pattern line a ½" (1.3cm) up from the bottom of the of the egg. Holding the carving upside down, start from this pattern line and make even, shallow cuts all the way around the carving to taper the bottom of the egg. Repeat two more times, with each series of cuts starting about halfway between your previous cuts and the bottom of the carving. Be careful not to remove too much in this step. You want the bottom rounded, but remember the bottom of an egg is wider than the top.

Undercutting

Steps 6 and 11 of this project use a technique called undercutting. To undercut an area, slide the tip of the blade underneath the area that will be removed, and then gently slide the tip back out. Be careful not to undercut too much or too little. This process works similarly to a stop cut, allowing you to cleanly cut off the area above the undercut.

5 Shape the beak. Starting at the horizontal centerline of the beak, carve an even, flat slope from the line to the top of the beak. Follow the same process to angle the bottom of the beak.

6 Finish the beak. Use the pencil to draw vertical and horizontal center lines across the beak. Undercut one corner of the beak by sliding the tip of your knife underneath the area along the corner and sliding it back out without removing any wood. Next, starting from the center of the beak, carve a flat surface between the horizontal and vertical pattern lines on that corner of the beak. Follow the same process on the other three corners to finish the beak.

7 Round the top of the head. Start alongside the beak and carve up toward the top, tapering the top of the carving with even cuts all the way around. Continue in regular intervals, until the top is completely rounded. Make deeper cuts in this step than you did when rounding the bottom, as you will need to round the entire top. As you round the area directly above the beak, try to leave a flat, smooth surface where the eyes will be painted.

8 Separate the top feathers. Use your pencil to draw a curve starting over the right eye area, running straight over the center of the head from front to back and then curving in the same direction on the back. Make a series of V-cuts along the line to separate the feathers from the head. Note that you will be cutting directly into and across the grain to make these cuts. Use the widest part of your blade as possible and make small, firm cuts as your blade will be pulled into the grain. After completing these cuts, flatten the area to the side of the feathers so that the features stand out above the head.

9 Finish the top feathers. Using the tip of the knife, add a series of small V-cuts across the ridge created in the previous step. Be careful to use only the very tip of the knife to avoid unwanted cuts across the head.

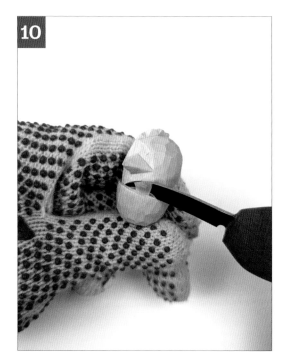

10 Separate the top of the eggshell. Redraw the horizontal pattern line ½" (1.3cm) above the bottom of the carving, and then make a stop cut along the entire line. Carve down to this stop cut, starting alongside the bottom edge of the beak, making even cuts around the entire carving. Repeat these cuts once more, starting closer to the shell, in order to further round the chick and separate it from the shell.

Blade Awareness

Blade awareness is a simple but important skill for beginner carvers to develop. It means being conscious of where the entire cutting edge of your blade is at all times. This may seem obvious, but it is easy to focus so much on one part of your blade that you lose track of where the rest of the blade is. This can lead to unwanted cuts and even damage to your carving. For example, in step 10 of this project, it would be easy to accidentally damage the beak with the back of your knife while carving the edges of the egg with the tip of your knife. Blade awareness also involves visualizing and sensing where the blade is when it is inside the wood and can't be seen, such as when cutting the triangles out along the edges of the egg (also in step 11). It takes practice, but specifically thinking about where the blade is as you make each cut will lead to making cleaner cuts and will become natural over time.

11 Carve the jagged edge of the shell.
Use the pencil to draw a series of triangular, jagged edges along the rim of the egg. These do not have to be even or symmetric. Use the tip of the knife to undercut one of the triangular areas marked for removal. Then, insert the tip of the knife alongside one side of the triangle and remove it. Finally, insert the tip along the other side of the triangle. The chip of wood inside the triangle should fall out. If it does not, repeat each cut until the wood comes out (do not pry). After completing the jagged edge around the entire shell, use the tip of your knife to gently smooth the hard edges along each triangle are that was removed.

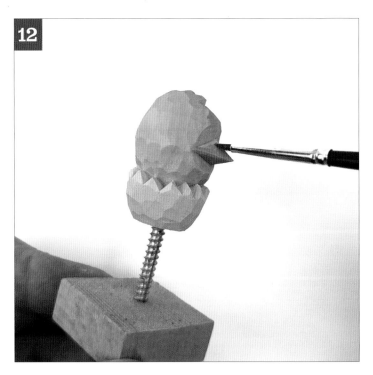

12 Paint. Start by painting the eggshell with a watered-down (50% water, 50% paint) white. You will need to use a small, detail brush to paint the edges of the shell. Next, paint the chick with a similarly watered-down paint of your desired color (e.g., yellow, light blue, or pink). Use a small detail brush to carefully paint the areas between the jagged edges of the egg and a larger round brush for the rest of the area. Finally, use the detail brush to paint the beak orange.

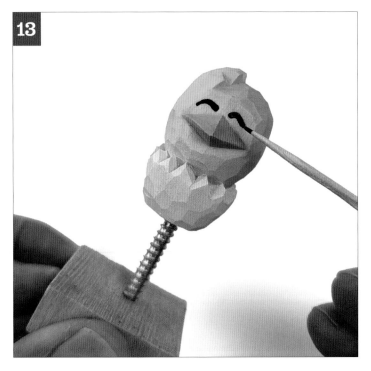

13 Add the eyes and finish. After the paint has dried, use a pencil to draw a pair of happy, arched-shaped eyes above the beak. Then, use a toothpick dipped into black paint to paint the eyes. Finish with a coat of Howard Feed-N-Wax.

Carving the Nest

These chicks are cute, but they look even better when sitting comfortably in their own little nest. Start with a piece of 1 ½" x 1 ½" (3.8 x 3.8cm) square basswood that is ¾" (1.9cm) tall, with the grain running vertically. Use a pencil and ruler to find and mark the center of the top of the wood.

1 Drill. Use a 1 ⅞" (48mm) Forstner bit to drill a hole in the center of the top of the carving to a depth of about ⅛" (3.2mm). If you don't have a Forstner bit, you can skip this step, and the chick can just set on top of the finished nest.

2 Round the sides. Use your knife to cut the hard corners off of the sides of the nest. Continue removing hard corners until the entire nest is rounded to a cylindrical shape (it should look like a circle when viewed from the top or bottom).

3 Round the bottom. Holding the nest upside down, use push cuts to round the bottom of the nest, taking care to taper evenly around the entire nest.

4 Smooth the corners. Use the tip of your knife to smooth the hard corners along the outside rim of the top of the nest, as well as the inside rim created by the drill bit in step 1.

5 Texture the nest. Using a V-tool, add horizontal V-cuts around the outside of the nest. Make cuts at slightly different angles and depths, overlapping alongside one another. If you don't have a V-tool, you may make V-cuts with a knife to complete this step.

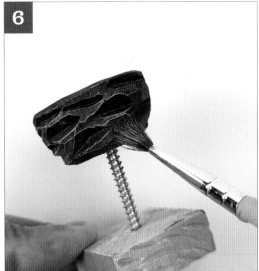

6 Paint. Use a flat brush to paint the nest with a lightly watered-down brown (25% water, 75% paint). After the paint has dried, lightly dry-brush the nest with white. Finish with a coat of Howard Feed-N-Wax.

Simple Wood Spirit

There is just something fun and satisfying about carving faces in wood. It's a subject that attracts new carvers to the hobby and keeps experienced carvers busy for years. I've designed this project for two purposes for beginners. The first is to provide a simple introduction to face carving. The second is to get more familiar with the V-tool. With a little practice, you can complete these in about 15 minutes, making them great for gifts and a good option for testing different painting/finishing techniques.

MATERIALS

- Basswood, ¾" x ¾" x 3" (1.9 x 1.9 x 7.6cm)
- Americana by DecoArt acrylic paint: Avocado, Royal Navy, Peacock Teal, Heritage Brick
- Americana by DecoArt antiquing solution: Walnut Gel Stain
- Howard Feed-N-Wax
- Paper towels

TOOLS

- Carving knife
- ¼" (6mm) 60-degree V-tool
- ⅛" (3mm) 60-degree V-tool (optional)
- Flat or round paintbrush
- Pencil

Pattern

Photocopy at 100%.

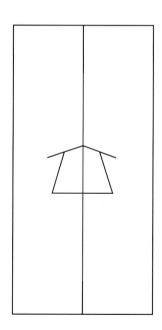

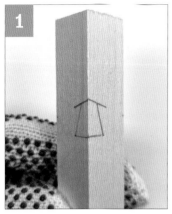

1 Apply the pattern. Draw the basic pattern lines for the nose and brows onto the carving. You will draw on the remaining reference lines on as you go. If you don't have any ¾" x ¾" (1.9 x 1.9cm) basswood, this project will scale perfectly to 1" x 1" x 4" (2.5 x 2.5 x 10.2cm) basswood when enlarging the pattern by 33 percent.

2 Separate the nose. Place a stop cut along the bottom of the nose and carve up to it. Continue until the width of the bottom of the nose is as wide as the pattern line.

3 Establish the eye sockets. Place horizontal stop cuts along the pattern lines for the brows, and carve up to them from about halfway up the nose. Be careful to keep your cuts symmetric so that the ridge along the center of the nose remains in line with the corner of the wood.

4 Round the forehead and mouth area. Flatten the hard corner directly above the nose by carving up from the brow. Continue to round the hard edges created by doing this until the front of the forehead is completely rounded. Follow a similar process to round the area underneath the nose.

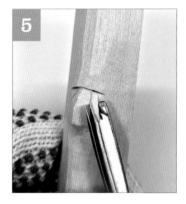

5 Shape the nose. Use your pencil to redraw the pattern lines for the sides of the nose. Use the tip of your knife to place a stop cut along the brow line, starting at the point where the pattern line for the nose runs into the brow. Then, use your V-tool to carve along the sides of the nose up toward the brow. If necessary, repeat the stop cut along the brow line to remove the chip created by the V-tool.

6 Finish the nose. Use the tip of your knife to undercut the bottom corners of the nose on each side, then cut off the hard corners at a 45-degree angle. Round the front and sides of the nose with your knife. Finally, use your V-tool to add a horizontal cut about a third of the way up on both sides of the nose.

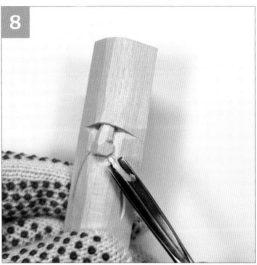

7 Finish the eyes. Deepen the eyes by carving up to the brow from halfway down the nose. Then, widen the eye sockets by extending the upper brow stop cut and carving up to it, until it extends about halfway from the existing cut to the edge of the carving. Finish the eyes by making a small, deep chip cut in the corner of each eye where the brow meets the nose.

8 Carve the smile lines. Draw the smile lines on with your pencil, then add a small stop cut at the point where the lines connect to the bottom/side of the nose. Carve the lines in with the V-tool, repeating the stop cuts if necessary to cleanly remove the wood. Use your knife to round any hard edges created by the V-tool.

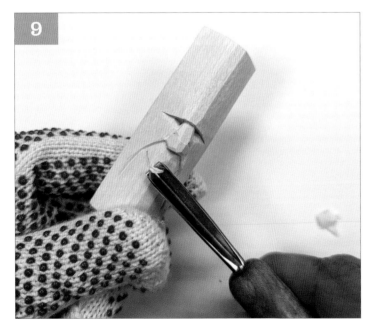

9 Carve the mouth and cheekbones. Draw the shape of the mouth with the pencil, and then carve it with the V-tool. Carve the cheek bones by making small cuts with the V-tool perpendicular to the smile line halfway between each side of the mouth and the nose.

Making Clean Cuts with Your V-tool

When cutting across the grain of the wood at an angle with a V-tool, the blade on one side is carving with the grain, while the other side is carving against it. This means cuts may be smooth on one side and a little rough on the other, especially when carving curves. If you end up with cuts that look rougher than you would like, try gently repeating the cut with your V-tool in the opposite direction, slightly tilting the tool toward the edge that was rougher in order to smooth it out.

10 Carve the eyebrows. Draw the eyebrows on with the pencil. Using the tip of your V-tool and being careful not to carve too deeply, carve the top outline of the eyebrow first and then carve three lines across the inside of the eyebrow area on each side. If preferred, you can use a smaller V-tool (⅛" [3mm]) for this step.

11 Separate the hair. Draw lines for the deep hairlines onto your carving with the pencil, and then carve them out with your V-tool. Make deep cuts and focus on making them wavy, not straight. Extend each of these cuts by making small V-cuts with your knife at the point where they run off the sides of the carving.

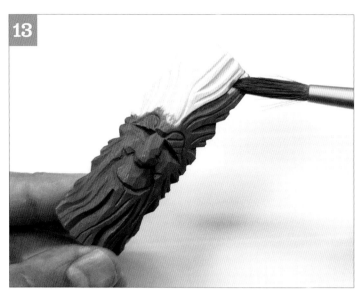

12 Finish the hair. Add shallow hairlines on the flat areas left between the larger lines created in the previous step. Use just the tip of your V-tool (or use a smaller ⅛" [3mm] tool). Focus on making the lines wavy and try to avoid multiple parallel lines.

13 Paint. Start the finishing process by using a large flat or round brush to paint the entire carving with watered-down (50% water, 50% paint) acrylic paint. Allow the paint to thoroughly dry. I used green in this example, but you can choose any color you want, and I encourage you to try a variety of colors.

14 Antique the carving. Use a large flat or round brush to apply slightly watered-down antiquing solution (about 75% solution and 25% water) over the entire carving. Gently wipe the excess antiquing solution off with a paper towel, being sure to leave the brown solution inside all of the crevices on the face. After drying completely, finish the carving with Howard Feed-N-Wax.

Alligator

While they lumber around like dinosaurs on land, alligators glide through the water with ease, leaving only their head, back, and tail sticking out of the water. This project attempts to capture the unique textures created by an alligator rising up out of the water. It is a good project for practicing carving flat, smooth surfaces and also making simple but effective texturing cuts. They are also pretty quick to carve, so after you finish one, you won't have to wait until later to carve another alligator.

Pattern

Photocopy at 100%.

TOP

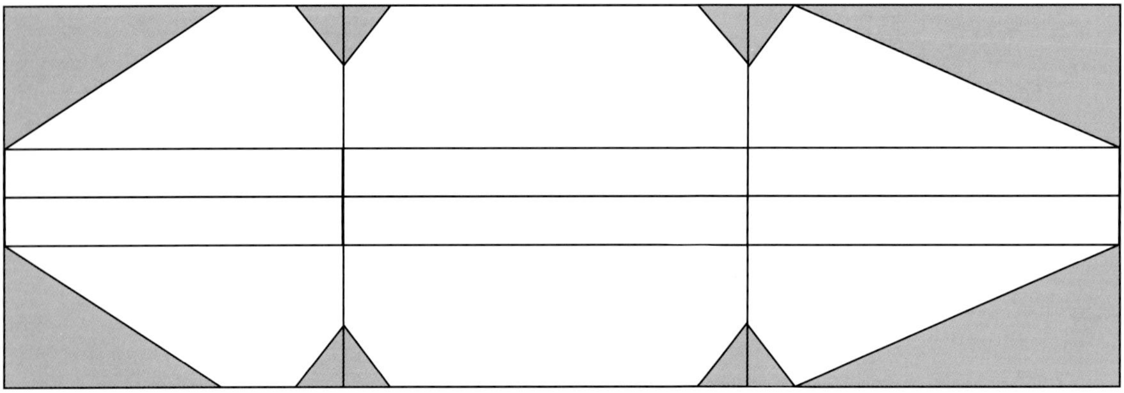

BOTTOM

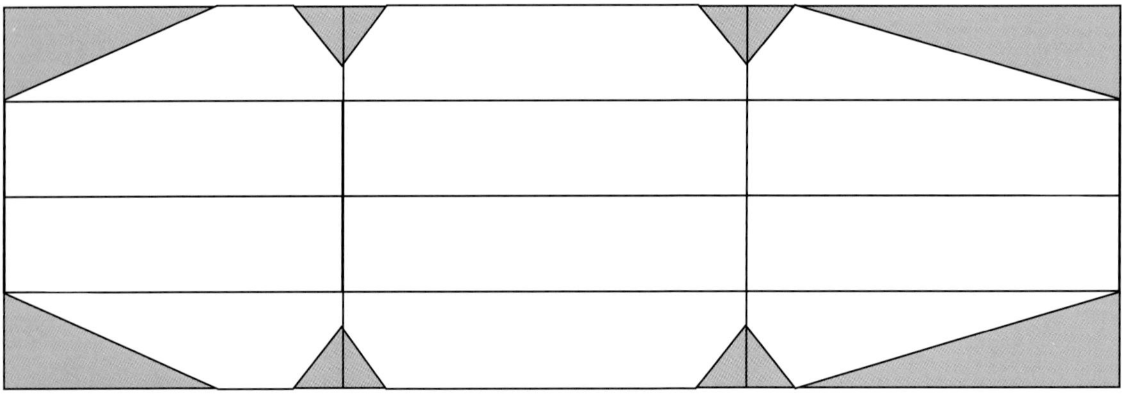

MATERIALS

- Basswood, ¾" x ¾" x 4 ½" (1.9 x 1.9 x 11.4cm)
- Americana by DecoArt acrylic paint: Avocado or Mulberry
- FolkArt acrylic paint: Vintage White
- Howard Feed-N-Wax

TOOLS

- Carving knife
- Pencil
- Ruler
- Flat paintbrush
- Detail knife (optional)

1 Apply the pattern. Use a pencil and ruler to draw the pattern onto the wood. Note that the top and bottom patterns both include two sides of the block, with each face measuring ¾" x 4½" (1.9 x 11.4cm). If you do not have any ¾" x ¾" (1.9 x 1.9cm) basswood, this pattern will scale perfectly to 1" x 1" x 6" (2.5 x 2.5 x 15.2cm) basswood when enlarged by 33 percent.

2 Shape the body. On the bottom of the alligator, completely flatten the area between the two long pattern lines that run the length of the bottom sides. The alligator will sit on this surface, so try to make it as flat as possible. Then, remove the ridge on the top of the alligator by flattening the top corner down to the two pattern lines running the length of the top. Finally, use the tip of the knife to lightly remove the hard corners on the sides of the alligator to a depth of about ⅛" (3.2mm).

3 Separate the head and tail. Use V-cuts to remove the shaded triangular areas from the sides of the alligator where the head and tail meet the body. Then, make additional V-cuts across the top of the alligator connecting these cuts and further separating the head and tail from the body. Extend the V-cuts similarly on the underside of the alligator down to the lower edge, but do not extend them all the way across the bottom.

4 Taper the head. Use push cuts to remove the large triangular shaded areas on either side of the head. Then, starting from the same distance back from the nose, taper the top and bottom of the head toward the center of the snout. Aim for smooth, flat surface on all four sides. When you are done, the remaining flat front of the snout should be about an ⅛" (3.2mm) tall and ¼" (6.4mm) wide.

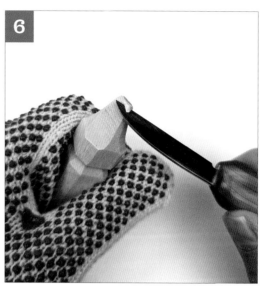

5 Finish shaping the head. Make additional cuts across the hard corners created between the sides and top/bottom of the head in the previous step. Then, go over each surface with a rolling cut, pushing the blade deeper into the wood by the head and then rolling up toward the nose. Check your work for symmetry as you go, trying to keep smooth even facets on each side. Narrow the sides of the head slightly so that the body will be slightly wider than the head.

6 Round the nose. Cut off the corners of each side of the nose, from just below the tip. Continue until the nose has been rounded across the tip, leaving no uncarved wood at the front of the nose.

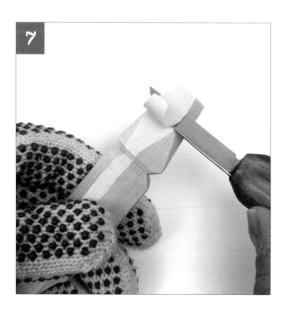

7 Taper the tail. Taper the tail by removing the large triangular shaded areas on either side of the tail. Then, angle the entire tail straight down along the back of the tail, until you have lowered the back of the tail to within ⅛" (3.2mm) from the bottom. Try to maintain smooth, flat surfaces on the sides and top of the tail in this process.

8 Finish the tail. Continue tapering the tail by making angled cuts across the hard corners created between the sides and top of the tail in the previous step. Then, shave down each surface until the tail comes to a point. Check your cuts for symmetry as you go and aim for making smooth, flat surfaces. Remember, the bottom of the tail will remain completely flat, so only carve in from the sides and down from the top to form the tip. Slightly narrow the outside edges of the tail and the top of the tail where it nears the body so that the body is slightly wider than the tail.

9 Texture the back. Using a smaller detail knife (or the tip of your larger knife), make a series of five, evenly spaced horizontal V-cuts across the back of the body of the alligator. You may want to draw these across the back with a pencil first. After making the initial cuts straight across the back, make additional V-cuts extending each cut down each side of the alligator.

10 Texture the head and tail. Make pairs of horizontal side-by-side V-cuts on the outside upper ridges of the tail. Make five evenly spaced rows of these V-cuts extending down the length of the tail. Then, add two similar pairs of V-cuts across the outside upper ridges of the flat area of the head.

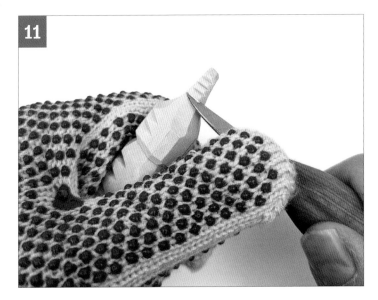

11 Carve the teeth. Make a series of small, vertical V-cuts along the sides of the head toward the nose.

12 Carve the eyes. Draw a horizontal line across the bottom of the eyes at the point where the snout is just starting to curve up towards the head. Then, draw two triangles side by side extending above this line. Use a chip cut to remove the triangle of each eye. Place the tip of knife in and out along each side of the eye, and then slide the tip of your blade gently across the bottom of the eye to remove the chip.

13 Paint. Use a flat brush to paint the entire alligator with a heavily watered-down (75% water, 25% paint) green or another color of your choosing (I recommend purple for a fun variation). Allow the paint to dry thoroughly, then use a round brush with undiluted white paint to lightly dry-brush the ridges along the center of the tail, back, and head as well as the tooth and eye areas. Finish with a coat of Howard Feed-N-Wax.

Roughing vs. Detail Knives

If you don't have both a roughing knife and a detail knife yet, don't worry, this project is still very doable with just one knife. However, if you have more than one carving knife, then it is good to think about when to use each knife to your advantage. In this project, I chose to demonstrate this by using a roughing knife with a blade length of about 1 ¾" (4.5cm) for steps 1 through 8 and a detail knife with a blade length of about 1 ¼" (3.2cm) for steps 9 through 11. When carving the large, flat surfaces used in shaping the alligator, the larger roughing blade is ideal. It allows me to make those large, smooth surfaces with fewer cuts, which helps ensure I get completely flat surfaces and maintain symmetry. For steps 8 through 12, the smaller detail knife is ideal for cutting the narrow V-cuts, and I especially appreciate the thinner blade when making the chip cuts for the eyes.

Goldfish

If you spend any time at a woodcarving show or browsing through woodcarving communities online, you will find that fish—ranging from small and simple to large and lifelike—are a very common subject for woodcarvers. I designed this fish to be a simple option for beginners to make their first fish. The basic shape is here, but you can use this as a template and add your own details or experiment with different shapes and sizes. After making a few, you too may get hooked on fish carving!

MATERIALS

- Basswood, 1" x 1" x 2" (2.5 x 2.5 x 5.1cm)
- FolkArt by Plaid acrylic paint: Pure Orange
- Howard Feed-N-Wax
- Toothpicks
- Eyelet or magnet (optional)
- Superglue (optional)

TOOLS

- Carving knife
- ⅛" (4mm) U-gouge
- Pencil
- Ruler
- Flat paintbrush
- Woodburner (optional)

Pattern

Photocopy at 100%.

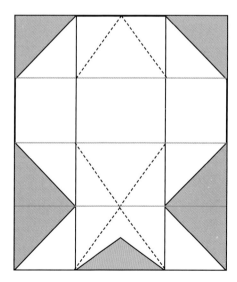

1 Apply the pattern. Flatten the block of wood by drawing vertical center lines on each face of the block, and then using your knife to remove the entire front and back corner between these vertical lines(see sidebar on page 32). Then, use a pencil and ruler to draw on the pattern. Use the same pattern for the front and back of the block. The dotted pattern lines are used as reference and can be drawn on as you go along.

2 Rough out the shape. Use push cuts to remove the shaded portions of the pattern to shape the top of the fish's head. Then, make a series of deep V-cuts to remove the shaded areas on either side of the tail.

3 Shape the sides of the head. Use the pencil to draw the dotted pattern lines on the front and back of the fish. Draw a centerline along the outside edges of the head. Use your knife to completely flatten the area between the dotted pattern line and centerline along the side of the head. Repeat on all four corners. When you are done, the top of the wood (where the point of the nose will be) will look like a diamond, or square shape.

4 Taper the head. Use your pencil to draw a centerline from top to bottom across the flat area where the nose of the fish will be. Then, starting ½" (1.3cm) down from the tip of the nose, make a series of push cuts to carve the flat side of the fish up at a constant angle to the centerline. Repeat on the opposite side of the fish. Carve right up to, but not over the centerline from each direction.

5 Smooth the corners around the head. Use the tip of your knife to gently shave the hard edge off the sides and front of the head.

6 Shape the sides of the body and tail. Use your pencil to draw on the diagonal dotted pattern lines leading from the body to the tail of the fish. Also, draw a centerline along the sides of these sections of the fish. Place a deep stop cut at the point where the body connects to the tail, and then make a series of V-cuts into this stop cut to flatten the side of the body and the side of the tail to the point where they meet. The body/tail should pinch in and meet right at the center of the side of the fish. Repeat on all four corners of the fish.

7 Taper the tail. Use the pencil to draw a centerline from top to bottom along the flat surface of the tail of the fish. Then, starting at the point where the body meets the tail, use a series of push cuts to taper the tail at a consistent angle from this point to the centerline of the tail. Repeat the process on the opposite side.

Practicing on Scrap Wood

It can be nerve-wracking to make a new cut for the first time on a carving that you have already invested a lot of time with. When carving, it can be helpful to have a piece or two of scrap wood handy for trying out a cut before attempting it on your actual carving. Examples from this project might be trying an against-the-grain V-cut on the end of a piece of wood to get a feel for it before making the cut in step 8. Or you may want to try the cuts to make the scales with a U-gouge on the flat side of a scrap piece of wood before making the cuts on the real thing.

Carving Against the Grain

Although you should avoid it as much as possible, there will be time when you have to carve against the grain in order to make a cut. When you have to carve against the grain, you will feel your knife get pulled into the wood, making it easy to break the wood or make a larger cut than you intended. To avoid this, use a firm grip and start with smaller cuts, taking multiple passes to get the depth required. A small, thin blade may struggle to make these cuts, so try to use the widest part of your blade possible, not the fragile tip that you use for details. It's also a good idea to strop your knife before and/or after cutting against the grain, as these cuts will dull your blade more quickly than normal cuts.

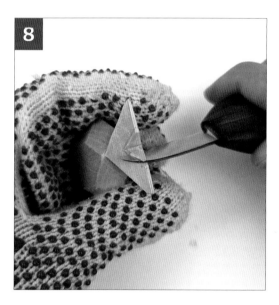

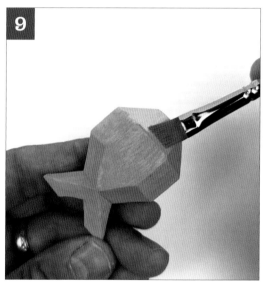

8 Finish the tail. Use your pencil to draw the pattern lines to indicate the area to be removed at the bottom of the tail. Place a stop cut in the center of the tail, and then make progressively deeper V-cuts to remove the area. Note that your knife will slide easily in on the stop cut because it is going directly into the grain of the wood. Start with small, deliberate cuts for your V-cuts and get gradually larger as you will be carving against the grain in this step. When you are done, use the top of your knife to gently smooth the outside edges of the tail, similar to the process used in step 5.

9 Paint the fish. Use a flat brush to paint the fish with heavily watered-down (75% water, 25% paint) orange acrylic paint (or the desired color of your choice). Allow the paint to dry.

10 Carve the scales. Each of the scales is carved by sticking a ⅛" (4mm) U-gouge directly into the wood to make a stop cut, then moving back ¹⁄₁₆" to ⅛" (1.6 to 3.2mm) and making a push cut with the gouge up to the stop cut. Start with one scale in the center near the front, then place one on either side of it. Next, add the two scales in the center row and finally one in back. If you don't have a U-gouge, you can use a V-tool for a similar effect, make chip cuts with your knife, woodburn scales on the sides, or just skip this step.

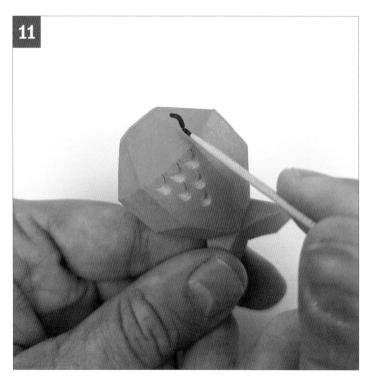

11 Paint the eyes and finish the carving. Use a pencil to draw in happy eyes on each side of the head, and then use a toothpick dipped in black paint to paint each eye. Finish the carving with a coat of Howard Feed-N-Wax. The flat nature of these fish lends themselves to either mounting a magnet on one side or adding an eyelet on the top to turn into an ornament or accessory in a larger scene.

Seashell

The overall process and techniques used for carving this shell are a great example of taking the skills and techniques developed from previous projects and applying them to make something new. There are a lot of things you can do with the finished products—they work well as magnets, pendants, keychains, or just standalone shells on a desk or shelf. So don't be shell-fish—carve a bunch and give them away!

MATERIALS	TOOLS
• Basswood, 1" x 1" x 1 ½" (2.5 x 2.5 x 3.8cm)	• Carving knife
• FolkArt by Plaid acrylic paint: Plantation Rose, Sky Mist, Vintage White	• Ruler
	• Flat paintbrush
	• Round paintbrush
• Howard Feed-N-Wax	• Pencil
• Eyelet (optional, for hanging shell)	• V-tool (optional)
• Magnet (optional)	
• Superglue (optional)	

Pattern

Photocopy at 100%.

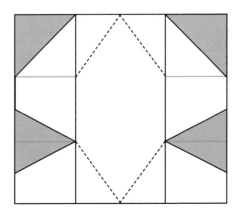

1 Apply the pattern. Flatten the block of wood by drawing vertical center lines on each face of the block, and then using your knife to remove the entire front and back corner between these vertical lines (see sidebar on page 32). Then, use a pencil and ruler to draw the pattern on the front and back of the wood.

2 Rough out the shape. Make a series of progressively deeper V-cuts to remove the shaded areas on each side of the bottom of the shell. Then, use a series of push cuts to remove the shaded area from the sides of the top of the shell.

3 Shape the top. Use your pencil to draw the dotted pattern lines on the front and back of the shell. Draw a centerline along the sides of the shell toward the top. Use your knife to completely flatten the area between the dotted pattern line and centerline along the side. Repeat on all four corners. When you are done, the top of the shell should have flat diamond/square shape remaining.

4 Taper the top. Use a series of push cuts to tapper the front of the shell toward the top, starting about ¼" (6.4mm) down from the top. Taper the back of the shell similarly, until the front and back meet and create a center ridge across the top of the shell.

5 Shape the bottom. Draw the dotted pattern lines on the front and back of the bottom part of the shell. Use push cuts to flatten the area between these pattern lines and the sides of the shell. When you are done, when viewed from the bottom, the shell will look like a wide, narrow diamond shape.

6 Taper the bottom. Use a series of push cuts to taper the front of the bottom of the shell toward the bottom. Start at the same position as the cuts in the previous step, ½" (1.3cm) up from the bottom. Taper the back of the shell similarly, until they meet and create a center ridge across the bottom edge of the shell.

7 Separate the wings of the shell. Use your pencil to redraw the dotted pattern lines on the front and back of the bottom of the shell. Place a deep stop cut along this line, and then make a series of cuts across the wings of the shell into this stop cut. Continue until you have extended the cuts about halfway across each wing.

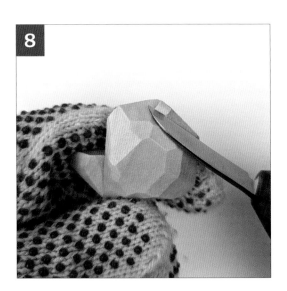

8 Smooth the hard edges. Use the tip of your knife to smooth the hard corners created on the sides of the bottom of the shell that were created in the last step. Pay attention to the position of the tip of your knife and take care not to accidentally cut into the wings of the shell. Then, carve over any hard edges and corners remaining on the front and back of the shell. Finally, smooth the corners along the outside edges of the shell and across the top.

9 Shape the wings. Round the outside edges of the wings and remove the outside corners to make them slightly smaller. Then, holding the shell upside down, make a small V-cut on either side of the point where the wings meet the center bottom of the shell. These cuts will be directly against the grain so take care to make small, controlled cuts.

Making Long V-Cuts With the Grain

The V-cuts made in step 10 of this project are much longer than those used in previous projects in this book, but they are also different because in some areas they are running along the grain instead of across the grain. To make a long V-cut along the grain, start by placing the length of the cutting edge of your knife directly into the location of the cut and push in to create a stop cut. Then, cut into this stop cut with the length of your knife from the same angle on both sides. You may find that the wood breaks off in long thin fibers if your cuts don't line up exactly. You can repeat the cuts a few times to clean them up, if needed. That said, these kinds of long V-cuts are very easy to do with a V-tool. If you have one available, you could choose to complete these cuts with a V-tool instead, which should glide evenly through the wood and leave nice, uniformly shaped V-shaped lines in your wood.

10 Texture the shell. Use the pencil to draw four lines across the front and back of the shell. The lines should each start at the bottom center of the shell and extend out to divide the shell into roughly five equal sections. To carve each of these lines, start by making a long V-cut across the center of the line. Then, extend the cut, with additional V-cuts toward the bottom of the shell. Make these cuts narrower as you go, so your lines don't overlap as they near each other toward the bottom of the shell. Then, extend each cut similarly toward the top, taking care to ensure that the lines on the front and back of the shell align and run into each other over the top.

11 Shape the outside edges of the shell. Make a large V-cut on the outside edges of the shell where each line from the previous step connects from the front to the back of the shell.

12 Texture the wings. Add three small V-cuts along the face of each wing of the shell. Start with one in the middle, running roughly parallel to the side of the shell. Then, make a smaller cut on each side. You will need to hold your carving and knife carefully in this step, taking care to support the wing so that it does not break off. Start with small cuts and make them larger, if needed, taking care not to push too hard into the wood.

13 Paint and finish. Use a flat brush to paint the shell with a heavily watered-down (75% water, 25% paint) acrylic paint of your choice. I used a light blue and light pink. Allow the paint todry, and then use a round brush to heavily dry-brush the whole carving with white paint. Finish with a coat of Howard Feed-N-Wax. If desired, add an eyelet to use the shell as a pendant. You could also add a magnet at this time.

Design Inspiration

I often get asked where I get ideas for new carving designs. One answer is that, for me, it is similar to finding shapes in the clouds in the sky. However, instead of staring at clouds, I find myself looking at my carvings and seeing different objects in the shapes I've made. Sometimes, I intentionally carve abstract patterns and shapes and see what objects they bring to mind. Other times, I see different objects in the shapes of my finished carvings. For example, an upside-down Christmas tree can become a nice potted plant. In this case, if you hold the shell in this project horizontally, you may notice that it has some striking similarities to the Goldfish project in this book. (I actually got the idea for this shell while working on my fish design. A few adjustments and iterations later, and I transformed my fish design into a shell.) Pay attention to the shapes you are making as you carve—you never know what you might find to carve next!

Grumpy (or Happy) Cat

It's easy to see how the grumpy cat became one of the internet's most popular memes. There is something amusing about the cat that simply is never amused. This project is a fun introduction to carving an animal face with some cartoon characteristics. The process provides a lot of practice with making small, detailed cuts, but you can also choose a simpler carve and experiment with other expressions by following the provided modifications for the happy cat. Give them a try, and you're sure to be feline good after spending some time making these grumpy (or happy) faces.

MATERIALS

- Basswood, 1" x 1" x 1 ½" (2.5 x 2.5 x 3.8cm)
- FolkArt by Plaid acrylic paint: French Gray, Camel, Pure Black, Vintage White
- Howard Feed-N-Wax
- Toothpick

TOOLS

- Carving knife
- Pencil
- Ruler
- Flat paintbrush
- Detail paintbrush

Pattern

Photocopy at 100%.

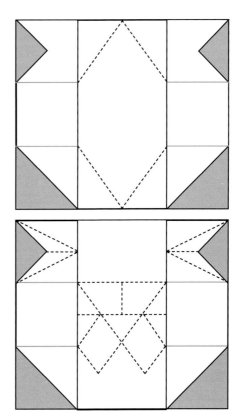

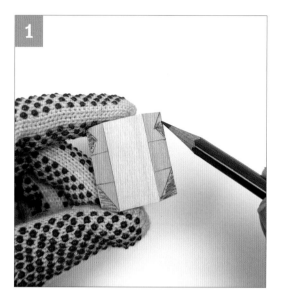

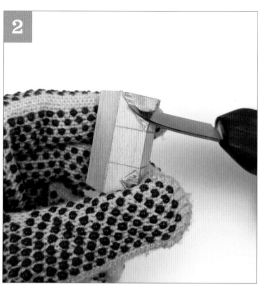

1 Apply the pattern. Flatten the block of wood by drawing vertical center lines on each face of the block, and then using your knife to remove the entire front and back corner between these vertical lines (see sidebar on page 32). Then, use a pencil and ruler to draw the pattern on the front and back of the wood. The second pattern shows the layout for the face and can be drawn on just the front of the carving as you go along.

2 Cut off the bottom corners. Holding the carving with the bottom pointing up, use push cuts to remove the shaded triangular areas on either side of the bottom of the head.

3 Angle the bottom of the head. Draw a centerline along the outside edges of the bottom of the head (the surface you carved in the previous step). Then, draw the dotted pattern lines from the general pattern onto the front and back of the wood. Use your knife to completely flatten the area between these two lines. Repeat on all four corners. When you are done, the bottom of the wood will look like a diamond, or square shape.

4 Taper the bottom of the head.
Draw a centerline running side-to-side across the bottom of the wood. Then, still holding the carving with the bottom facing up, carve up to this line from ¼" (6.4mm) down on the front and back of the carving. Try to make a consistent, flat surfaces that meet at a single ridge along the bottom of the head.

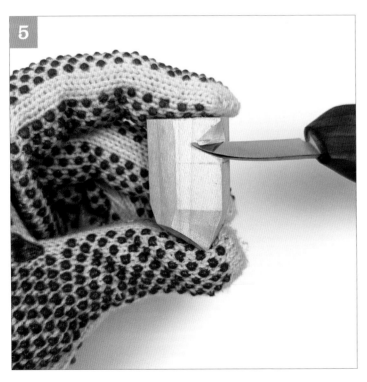

5 Separate the ears. Holding the carving with the top of the head up, make a series of progressively deeper V-cuts to remove the shaded pattern areas defining the shape of the ears. Note that these areas can be fragile (which is why it's a good idea to start by shaping the bottom the head). Be aware of the protruding ears, and be careful how you hold your carving as you continue carving.

6 Angle the top of the head. Draw the angled pattern lines from the general pattern across the front and back of the head. Then, cut at an angle between this line and the outside corners of the top of the head. This is similar to the cut in step 2, but will result in a wider diamond shape remaining on the top of the head because of the ears.

7 Taper the top of the head. Draw a centerline running side-to-side across the top of the head. Carve up to this line from ¼" (6.4mm) down on the front and back of the carving. Just as in step 4, aim for consistent, flat surfaces that meet at a single ridge along the top of the head.

8 Define the nose and cheeks. Draw the pattern lines defining the top of the nose and cheeks onto the front of the wood. Make a horizontal stop cut all the way across the front of the wood, along the line for the top of the nose. Carve down to this from the brow line, repeating until the top of the nose extends back to a depth of about ¹⁄₁₆" (1.6mm). Then, make stop cuts on the angled lines along the tops of the cheeks. Carve into these from the outside, until they connect at the same depth as the top of the nose. Making the connection between these two surfaces smooth requires some precision, so use shallow cuts in this step to avoid over-cutting and creating unwanted lines.

9 Define the nose and mouth. Draw the remaining pattern lines defining the nose and cheeks. This effectively makes an X shape with the nose on top, the mouth on bottom, and the cheeks on the sides. Make a stop cut across both lines of the X, and then make a shallow V-cut by carving into them slightly from both sides.

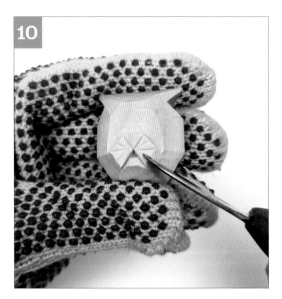

10 Carve the mouth and whiskers. Deepen the cuts running along the sides of the mouth. Then, make a triangle chip cut at the top of the mouth area to open the mouth. Make three small V-cuts across each cheek to make the whiskers.

11 Shape the head. Add a series of V-cuts around the outer edge of the cat's head. Place two evenly-spaced cuts on each of the outer sides, angled sides and bottom of the head, for a total of 10 V-cuts. These cuts are about ⅛" (3.2mm) deep and wide, but can vary to create a more jagged or rounded appearance as desired. Finally, make a large V-cut into the top of the head, right in the center between the two ears. Note that the V-cuts on the bottom and top of the head will be carved against the grain so start small, be careful, and be sure your knife is sharp.

12 Finish the ears. Draw the remaining pattern lines for the ears and follow these lines to taper the top of the head and front of the ears into each other, extending the ears further toward the center of the head. The end result will be an almost vertical surface for the front of the ears. Make a triangle chip cut in this flat surface on the front of each ear. Start by inserting and removing the tip of your knife along the sides of the triangle, and then remove the chip by cutting across the bottom of the triangle.

13 Carve the eye area. Draw the pattern lines on for the eyes. Make a long, shallow V-cut along the upper brow line. Then, make similar V-cuts along the sides of the eyes, connecting down to the corner of the nose from each side. To carve the centerline separating the two eyes, first make a stop cut along this line by drawing the tip your knife straight along the line. Then, angle the tip of your knife and make a similar line along your initial cut from both sides, so that they meet along the first line and make a V-shaped cut down the center of the eye area.

14 Carve the eyes. Make small, triangle chip cuts centered at the top of each eye, right at the brow line. Insert and remove your knife along the sides of the triangles, and then slide the tip of the knife across the base of the triangle (at the brow line) to remove the chip.

Make a Happy Cat

If you want to add some variety to the expression of your cat or simplify your carving process, consider carving a happy cat instead. To carve a happy cat, you can completely skip steps 13 and 14 and leave the eye area completely flat. Then, in step 15, angle the eyebrows up instead of down. Paint your happy cat your desired color (I chose orange), and then paint on simple happy eyes. If you are looking for other ways to simplify the carving, you could consider painting the center of the ears instead of carving them, and you could even paint on the mouth and whiskers instead of carving them.

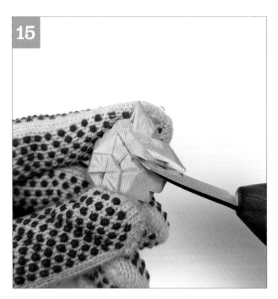

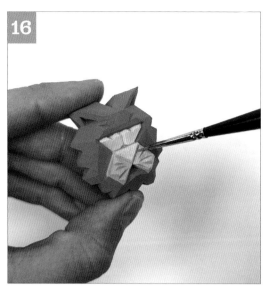

15 Add the eyebrows. Make small V-cuts angling down just above the upper corner of each eye and below the ears.

16 Paint. Paint the head with a watered-down (50% water, 50% paint) gray, using a small detail brush around the borders of the eyes and cheeks and a wide flat brush on the rest of the head. Then, use a small detail brush to paint the cheeks and eye areas with similarly watered-down tan and white paints. Use a toothpick dipped in undiluted black to add a dot at the center of each eye.

17 Dry-brush and finish. Use a round brush and an undiluted white paint to heavily dry-brush the outside edges of the cat and the cheeks. Lightly dry-brush over the ears and forehead area and avoid dry-brushing over the eyes and nose. Use a fine-detail brush to paint the nose an undiluted black (it's difficult to dry-brush without getting white on the nose, so keeping the nose for last will likely save you from having to repaint it). Finish with a coat of Howard Feed-N-Wax. For display, I recommend adding a magnet on the flat back of the cat.

Super Simple Gnomes

Gnomes have become such a popular subject in the carving world that it seems no book for beginning woodcarvers would be complete without a gnome project. This little gnome pattern is designed to be a simple option, providing the instantly recognizable hat, nose, and beard that make carving gnomes so fun. While these are simple, there is lot of room for customizing and adding details to these so be sure to try a few and have fun making your own variations. With a little practice and some imagination, there's gno limit to what you might create!

MATERIALS

- Basswood, 1" x 1" x 2" (2.5 x 2.5 x 5.1cm)
- FolkArt by Plaid acrylic paint: Christmas Red, Pale Gray, Uniform Blue, French Gray, Skyline, Vintage White
- Americana by DecoArt acrylic paint: Espresso
- Howard Feed-N-Wax

TOOLS

- Carving knife
- Fine-detail paintbrush
- Round paintbrush
- Flat paintbrush
- Pencil/pen
- Ruler

Pattern

Photocopy at 100%.

FRONT

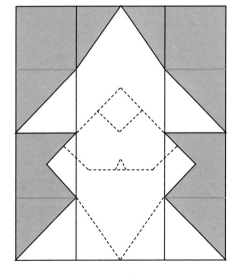

BACK

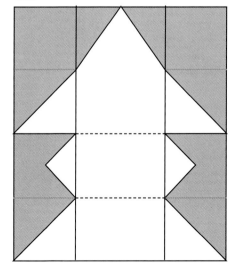

1 Apply the pattern. Flatten the block of wood by drawing vertical center lines on each face of the block, and then using your knife to remove the entire front and back corner between these vertical lines (see sidebar on page 32). Then, use a pencil and ruler to draw the front and back patterns on to the block of wood. If you choose to create a two-sided gnome (as described in step 9), you can use the front pattern on both sides of your block.

2 Rough out the main shape. Remove the wood indicated by the shaded portions of the pattern. On each side, start by placing a stop cut under the brim of the hat and carving up to it to remove the area between the top of the beard and the bottom of the hat. Then, turn the carving around and make a series of progressively larger V-cuts to remove the area between the beard and the legs. Finally, carve off the shaded portion on the side of the hat. For each step, make multiple cuts, but try to finish with flat surfaces on each area you remove.

3 Carve the point of the hat. Use the pencil to re-draw/extend the pattern lines for the brim off the hat, then draw a vertical centerline along both sides of the hat, up to the point at the top. Use push cuts to carve off the ridge between the centerline and your pattern line for the brim of the hat, until the area between these two lines is completely flat. Then, complete the same process from the other side of the hat. This process will leave a vertical ridge on the center of the front of the hat. Repeat the process on the back of the hat.

4 Establish the brim of the hat. Make stop cuts along the inside brim of the hat, from the tip of the center to the bottom of each side. Use push cuts to carve into these stop cuts to establish the brim of the hat. Be careful to make small, controlled cuts to avoid breaking the edge of the brim.

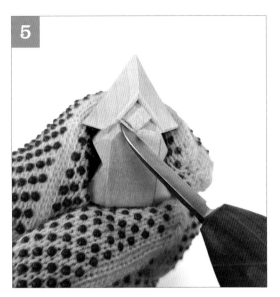

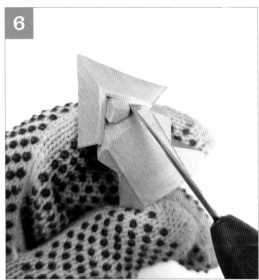

5 Carve the nose. Use the tip of your knife to make a small chip cut at the point where the top of the nose meets the brim of the hat. Then, make a larger chip cut on the bottom of each side of the nose. Do this by laying your blade along the side of the nose and inserting the tip of your knife deeply at the point where the nose meets the hat. Make a similar cut along the edge of the brim, inserting your knife tip deeply at the same point. Then, make a horizontal cut between these two cuts to remove a large triangle chip under each side of the nose.

6 Round the nose. Cut the sharp corner off from the bottom of the nose by making a small V-cut centered at the bottom of the nose. Gently slope the upper portion of the moustache into the bottom of the nose when you do this. Then, undercut the sharp corners on sides of the nose with the tip of your knife and cut the sharp corners off of each side of the nose. Smooth any remaining hard edges around the sides of the nose.

7 Define the beard. Make a deep stop cut along the pattern line for each side of the bottom of the beard, and then carve into it from about halfway across the leg area. Repeat this process to make a deep separation between the legs and each side of the beard. Then, use the tip of your knife to round over the hard edge created on the sides of the beard.

8 Carve the moustache. Separate the moustache from the beard by making two long V-cuts for the sides of the moustache. Then, make a long horizontal V-cut to connect these cuts along the bottom of the moustache. Finish the moustache by making a small chip-cut in the center of the bottom of the moustache.

9 Finish the back. Add simple features to finish the back by making two horizontal V-cuts along the back, one defining the bottom of the brim of the hat and the other separating the hair from the body. Alternatively, you may choose to complete steps 4 through 8 on the back of the gnome to carve a second face. This can be a fun option to experiment with some other designs and make a two-sided gnome.

10 Slope and wrinkle the hat. Add a slope to each side of the hat by using a rolling push cut. Starting just above the brim on the side of the hat, push your knife in at a steep angle, then roll up, tapering your cut so that your knife comes out just at the point of the hat. Repeat the cut on the ridge on the other side, as well as those on the center front and back of the hat. Add small V-cuts along the ridges on the sides of the hat to add some wrinkles.

Go Further?

After step 9, you could consider your gnome complete. The remaining steps are all optional and provide some ideas for adding additional detail and customization for your gnomes. Feel free to experiment with your own ideas to add character and detail as well.

11 Texture the beard. Make two to three large V-cuts on each side of the beard and make a small chip cut at the base of these V-cuts where the beard meets the legs. Then make smaller V-cuts in between each large cut. Follow a similar process to texture the sides of the mustache.

12 Define the legs. Use a push cut to remove the outer half off each leg so that the legs extend vertically down from the beard instead of out at an angle away from the body. Next, make a deep V-cut right where the inside of the leg meets the beard on each side to further separate the legs from the beard. Finally, add a small horizontal V-cut on each leg, just above the base of the carving to give an impression of feet.

13 Paint and finish. Use slightly watered-down acrylic paints (50% water, 50% paint) to paint the hat, beard, and legs. Use a fine-detail brush to paint the border areas, and then use a round or flat brush to paint the larger areas. For a more traditional look on a basic version of the gnome, use red for the hat, light gray for the beard, and blue for the legs. For a more rugged look on the textured gnome, use brown for the hat, gray for the beard, and a pale blue for the legs. Leave the nose unpainted.

14 Texture the beard. If you chose to add texture to your gnome's beard, use a round brush and white paint to dry-brush the beard area. Finish the carving with a coat of Howard Feed-N-Wax.

Butterfly

These cute and cheerful butterflies are sure to brighten your day, but they are also interesting to carve and will give your knife a serious workout. The flat shape of the wings means you will be removing a lot of wood, and there are several steps that involve cutting directly across or against the grain. Before you begin, you will want to make sure you start with a nice, sharp knife. After all, a sharp knife will cut wood like butter and make the chips fly!

MATERIALS

- Basswood, 1" x 1" x 2" (2.5 x 2.5 x 5.1cm)
- Americana by DecoArt acrylic paint: Peacock Teal, Cadmium Yellow
- FolkArt by Plaid acrylic paint: Eggplant, Plantation Rose, Pure Black, Sky Mist
- Howard Feed-N-Wax
- 20-gauge craft wire
- Wood glue or superglue
- Thick wire or wire coat hanger (optional)
- Toothpicks
- Small push pin
- Wooden dowel (optional)

TOOLS

- Carving knife
- Pencil
- Ruler
- Flat paintbrush
- Round paintbrush
- Fine-detail paintbrush
- Wire cutters
- Small needle-nose pliers
- Small embossing tool
- Drill with small bit (optional)

Pattern

Photocopy at 100%.

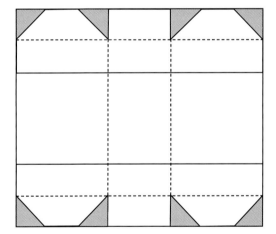

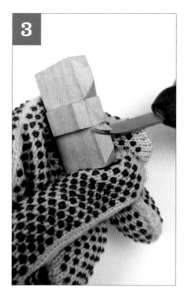

1 Apply the pattern. Flatten the block of wood by drawing vertical center lines on each face of the block, and then using your knife to remove the entire front and back corner between these vertical lines (see sidebar on page 32). Then, use a pencil and ruler to draw the pattern on the front and back of the wood. Note that the wood grain runs horizontally on this project, which is different than every other project in this book. References to horizontal/vertical in the instructions are relative to the orientation of the pattern, not the direction of the grain. So, vertical lines and cuts in these instructions will be across the grain and horizontal lines/cuts in this project will be with the grain.

2 Thin the wings. Make stop cuts along the side of the body, and then carve toward the body from the outside of each wing. Continue this process to gradually lower the wood until the wing area is completely flat, even with the horizontal pattern lines running along the top and bottom of the wings. Repeat the process on the front and back side of both wings.

3 Begin shaping the wings. Use push cuts to completely remove the shaded areas on the outside corners of the top and bottom of each wing. Then, use stop cuts and push cuts to remove the shaded areas on the inside corner of each wing where it meets the body.

4 Angle the outside corners of the wings. Cut off the outside corners from each wing, so that they angle down toward the edge of the wing. Use the pencil to draw a centerline along the outside edge along the corner of each wing (the area removed in the previous step). Then, draw a diagonal line across the front face of the wing, parallel to the line you just drew. Shade in the area between these two lines, as seen in the photo. Then, use your knife to completely flatten this shaded area. Repeat on the front and back side of the outside corners of each wing.

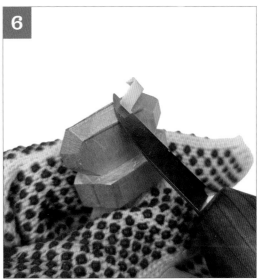

5 Angle the inside corners of the wings. Cut off the inside corners of each wing, so that they angle down toward the edge of the wing. Use the pencil to draw a centerline along the inside corner of each wing, where it slopes toward the body (the surface carved in the second part of step 3). Then, draw a diagonal line on the front face of the wing, parallel to the line you just drew. Make a stop cut where the body meets the wing in this area, and then use your knife to completely flatten the area between the two lines. Repeat the process on the front and back side of the inside corners of each wing.

6 Taper the wings. Use the pencil to draw a centerline along the outside edge of each wing. Then, draw a vertical line along the front and back of each wing, ⅛" (3.2mm) in from the outside edge of the wings. Use your knife to remove the area between these two lines. Note that you will be cutting directly across the grain, so be sure your knife is sharp, and you make a few passes to flatten the area. Repeat the process on the front and back of each wing.

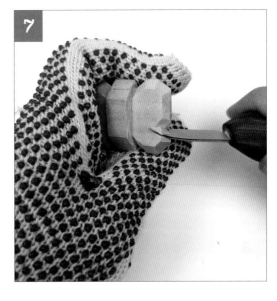

7 Notch the wings. Make a V-cut in the outside edge of each wing, about ½" (1.3cm) up from the bottom of each wing. The V-cut should extend down to about ⅛" (3.2mm) deep and ⅛" (3.2mm) wide. Be careful, as this notch will be carved directly against the grain. After making the initial V-cut, make diagonal cuts across the corners or the V-cut, extending the notch another ⅛" (3.2mm) deep. Add a second notch on the other wing.

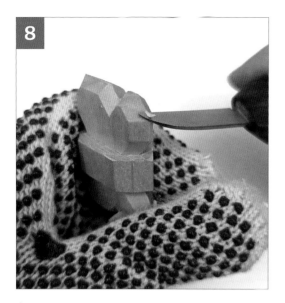

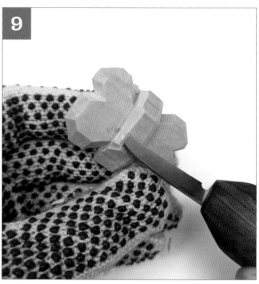

8 Smooth the outside edges of the wings. Use the tip of your knife to lightly smooth the hard corners left on the outside edges of each wing, leaving slightly flat surfaces along each outside edge.

9 Shape the body. Cut off the sharp edges along the sides of the body, until the shape of the body is rounded across the front and back. Be careful, as most of these cuts will be directly across the grain.

Checking for Symmetry

Carving for symmetry can be a challenge as it requires you to make repeated cuts at similar depths and angles. It takes practice to do this well, but it also takes a keen eye and an ability to adjust your cuts as you go along. It's a good idea to check your carving for symmetry as you go along. If you notice any differences, you can deepen a cut, or adjust an angle as needed to match the cut on the other side and maintain symmetry. Shaping the wings on this butterfly while maintaining symmetry can be a little tricky. The image here shows the shape of the wings after step 8. If you haven't already, this is a good point to stop and compare your wings to each other and to the picture. If you notice any differences, you can make some adjustments before moving on.

The carved butterfly wings are symmetric.

10 Separate the head. Draw a horizontal line to identify the bottom of the head, about ½" (1.3cm) down from the top of the head. Make a V-cut along this line to separate the head from the body. Then, remove a small triangle chip, centered on this line to further separate the side of the head from the body.

11 Deepen the top of the wings. Use stop cuts along the sides of the head, following by push cuts to extend the depth of the top of the wings so that they meet the body near the bottom of the head.

12 Finish the head and body. Make a shallow cut across the top of the head, lowering and flattening it slightly. Then, round the head by removing the hard corners on the top and bottom. Use a similar process to round the bottom of the body.

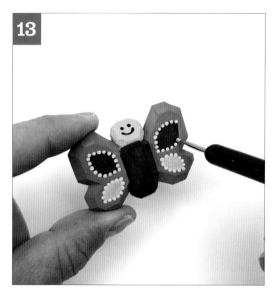

13 Paint the butterfly. Using watered-down (50% water, 50% paint) acrylic paints, use a flat brush to paint the wings teal and a round brush to paint the body dark blue and the head yellow. Allow the paint to dry thoroughly. Use a toothpick with undiluted black paint to paint on a smile and two small dots for the eyes. Use a small detail brush with undiluted paints to paint a purple leaf-shaped area in the upper area of each wing. Paint a similar shape using undiluted pink paint in the lower area of each wing. Finally, use a toothpick or a small embossing tool with undiluted light blue paint to add a dotted border around the pink and purple areas of the wings. Finish with a coat of Howard Feed-N-Wax.

14 Make the antennae. Cut a piece of 20-gauge (or similar) craft wire to a length of about 2" (5.1cm). Pinch the tip of one end of the wire with a small pair of needle-nose pliers, and then wrap the remaining wire around the pliers to bend the end of the wire into a spiral shape. Repeat for the second antenna, and then cut the straight ends to your desired length, ensuring both antennae are the same overall length.

15 Attach the antenna. Use a small push pin to punch pilot holes in the top of the head where the antenna will go in. Firmly push the antenna in the holes until they stick into the wood. For a stronger hold, dip the tip of the wire into wood glue or superglue before inserting.

Displaying your Butterfly

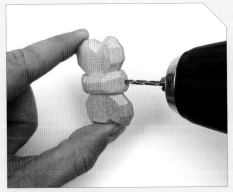

1 Drill a hole in the bottom of the butterfly.

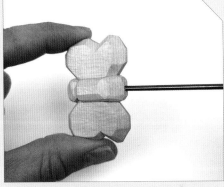

2 Insert the wire in the bottom of the butterfly.

3 A completed butterfly mounting on a wire.
There are several options for displaying your final butterfly. Hanging it is an obvious choice, but adding an eyelet to the top of the head can be tricky with the antennae already there. Mounting it on the end of a wire or dowel from the bottom is an easy solution that provides a few options for displaying. Begin by drilling a hole on the bottom end of the butterfly's body (you may want to do this prior to painting). Match the size of the drill bit to the size of the wire or dowel that you will use. Then, insert the wire or dowel into the butterfly. You may want to dip the tip into wood glue before inserting it for a stronger hold. Now, you can stick the other end into a potted plant, add it to a bouquet of flowers, or attach it to a wooden base, perhaps as part of a larger carved scene.

Pineapple

Aside from being delicious, pineapples are just a fun-looking fruit. The rough textures and spikes on both the pineapple and the stem create interesting textures that are just begging to be carved. In this project, you will find some familiar cuts and shapes used in previous projects, but you will also find some new techniques in the leaves and textures of the pineapple. Carving this pineapple is a real test of symmetry and precision, so take your time, carefully apply the pattern, and check your work as you go to ensure symmetry. Although you won't be able to eat them when you're done, these pineapples are a lot of fun to carve and will look great on display for years to come.

Pattern

Photocopy at 100%.

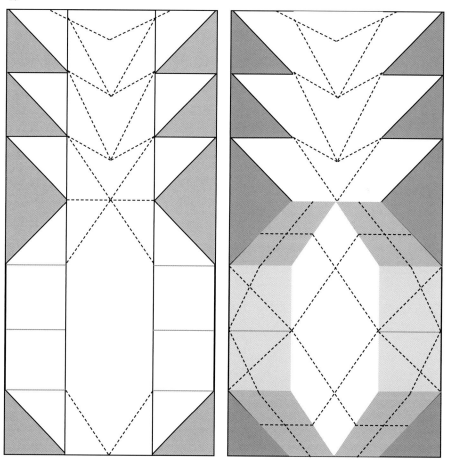

MATERIALS

- Basswood, 1" x 1" x 3 ½" (2.5 x 2.5 x 8.9cm)
- Americana by DecoArt acrylic paint: Cadmium Yellow, Avocado
- Howard Feed-N-Wax
- Wood glue (optional)

TOOLS

- Carving knife
- Pencil
- Ruler
- Flat paintbrush

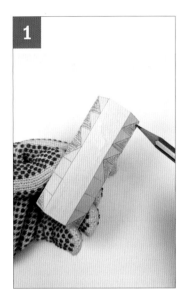

1 Apply the pattern. Flatten the block of wood by drawing vertical center lines on each face of the block, and then using your knife to remove the entire front and back corner between these vertical lines (see sidebar on page 32). Then, use a pencil and ruler to draw the pattern on the front and back of the wood. Note that the horizontal reference lines run in ½" (1.3cm) intervals and the dotted pattern lines across the front can be drawn on as you go. Use the general pattern to start. The second pattern shows the details of the pineapple texture and is used in step 14.

2 Rough out the shape. Use push cuts and V-cuts to remove the shaded areas of the pattern. To avoid breakage, carve each side of the pineapple from top to bottom.

3 Shape the bottom. Draw the dotted pattern lines on the front and back of the bottom of the pineapple and a centerline along the outside edges of the bottom. Use your knife to completely flatten the area between the dotted pattern line and centerline on the side. Repeat on all four corners. When you are done, the bottom of the pineapple will look like a diamond, or square shape.

4 Taper the top. Draw a horizontal centerline extending side to side across the top of the pineapple. Then, starting ¼" (6.4mm) down from the top, use push cuts to taper the front and back of the pineapple up to this centerline. Try to finish with a single, smooth surface on each side, tapering to a straight ridge across the top.

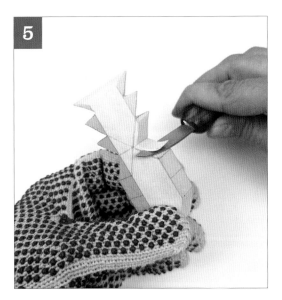

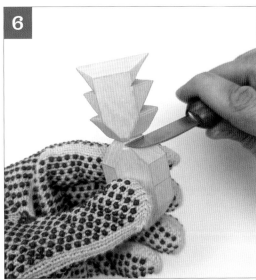

5 Shape the pineapple and stem. Draw the pattern lines making an X shape across the front and back of the carving where the top of the pineapple and bottom of the stem meet. Place a deep stop cut along the horizontal line along the center of one side of the X, and carve up and down to it until you have made a deep V-cut across the sides, pinching into the center of the X. The area between the pattern line and center of the outside edge of the carving should be completely flat when you are done. Repeat on all four corners.

6 Separate the pineapple from the stem. Make a series of small V-cuts centered on the line between the top of the pineapple and the bottom of the stem. These should extend about ⅛" (3.2mm) above or below the line and be made on each side, front and back of the carving.

7 Separate the stem tiers. Draw the pattern lines defining the edges of the tiers of the stem. Make stop cuts across these lines, and then make V-cuts along them, extending from the outside edge and ending where they meet at the center of the carving. Repeat on both sides.

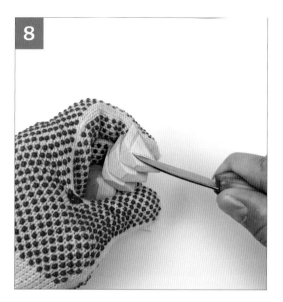

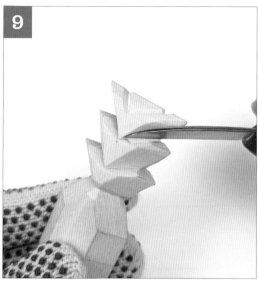

8 Separate the top. Draw the pattern lines for the wide V shape on the top of the pineapple stem. Then, make stop cuts along these lines and make V-cuts into these stop cuts. The cuts should meet on the front and back of the pineapple at the center and connect to each other across the top. Cut the hard corners off at the point where they meet over the top.

9 Angle the sides of the stem. Draw the remaining pattern lines on the front and back of the top two tiers of the stem, showing the angles extending from the top to bottom of each tier of the stem. Make cuts across the sides of the stem, angling the sides into the V on the bottom of each level. These angles should be the same as those made for the sides of the bottom tier of the stem in step 5. Repeat on both sides of the top two levels of the stem.

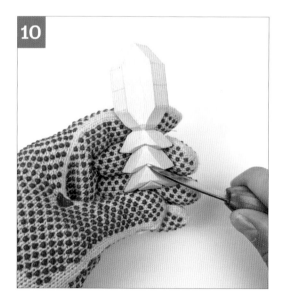

10 Separate the stem tiers. Remove a small triangle chip at the center of the base of the top two tiers of the stem, where they meet the tier below them. Repeat on both sides of the carving.

11 Finish the stem tiers. Starting on the bottom tier of the stem, make a V-cut extending the ridge along the top of the stem tier across the center and over the left side of the stem. Make a similar cut in the center tier but running from left to right. Then, make the same cut on the top tier again running right to left. Finally, use the tip of your knife to smooth the corners of the top edges of each tier of the stem.

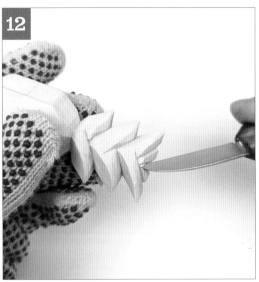

12 Finish the top of the stem. Make a wide, shallow V-cut directly into the center of the top of the stem. Be careful, as this will be cutting directly against the grain. Then, make a small V-cut, running from left to right at the base of the wide V you just carved into the top. Repeat on the other side.

13 Flare the sides of the stem. Holding the pineapple upside down, make rolling push cuts on the underside of each tier of the stem to curve the bottom of the stem leaves.

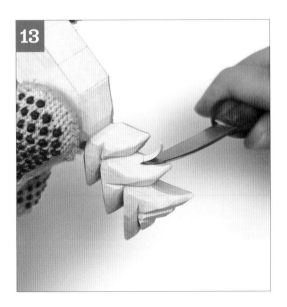

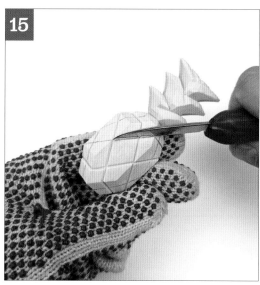

14 Draw the pattern lines on the pineapple. Using the detail pattern as a guide, carefully draw the pattern lines on the surface of the front and back of the pineapple. I find it easiest to make small dots with my pencil at the key points where lines will intersect each other or the sides of the carving. Then, use a ruler, or a steady hand, to connect the dots and draw the pattern lines onto the pineapple.

15 Carve the pineapple texture lines. Use the length of your knife to make V-cuts along each pattern line on the front and back of the pineapple. Start by making stop cuts on each line. Then, carve into them from either side of the line. A consistent depth is important so that the intersections remain smooth. I suggest starting with the lines in the center of the pineapple and working your way toward the outside, leaving the lines that meet on the outside edges for the end as these areas can become prone to breaking.

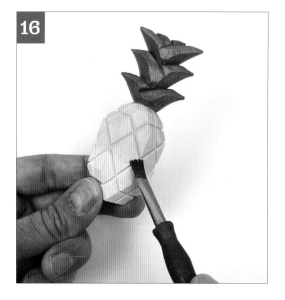

16 Paint and finish. Use a flat brush to paint the pineapple and stem with heavily watered-down (75% water, 25% paint) yellow and green acrylic paints. Finish with a coat of Howard Feed-N-Wax.

Repairing Broken Carvings

You can see a piece of wood breaking off a pineapple carving.

Glue is present on the broken piece of the carving, ready to reattach to the main carving.

Holding the glued piece in place while it dries.

If a piece of wood breaks off while you are carving, don't panic! It is usually very easy to repair with wood glue. In this case, I accidentally broke the tip of one of the tiers of the pineapple stem while carving. Place a dab of wood glue on the broken surface, and then place it back in the place where it broke off. Hold it firmly in place for several minutes and allow to dry for another 10 to 15 minutes before you try to carve the area again. It is usually pretty easy to smooth over any remaining cracks, and you can continue to carve that area (although I suggest you do so as lightly and carefully as possible). By the time you paint and finish, it's likely that you won't even notice where the break happened, and neither will anyone else!

Rose in Vase

Roses are red, violets are blue, I whittled a rose and now so can you! I love carving plants, including flowers. It's fun to try and capture their details and shapes with as few lines as possible. This project uses many cuts and shapes that you will recognize from previous projects to create the overall shape of a simple vase and rose, but it adds some variations in order to create the narrow stem and curved shapes of the leaves and rose bud. While the pattern and overall shape are pretty simple, the process involves removing a large amount of wood, and getting the smooth angles and surfaces right can take some practice and patience. Stick with it, and you will be rewarded with a simple, elegant rose that looks great on display and is also perfect for giving away.

MATERIALS

- Basswood, 1" x 1" x 4 ½" (2.5 x 2.5 x 11.4cm)
- FolkArt by Plaid acrylic paint: Skyline, Fresh Cut Grass, and Christmas Red
- Howard Feed-N-Wax

TOOLS

- Roughing knife, 1 ¾" (4.5cm)
- Pencil
- Ruler
- Flat paintbrush

Pattern

Photocopy at 100%.

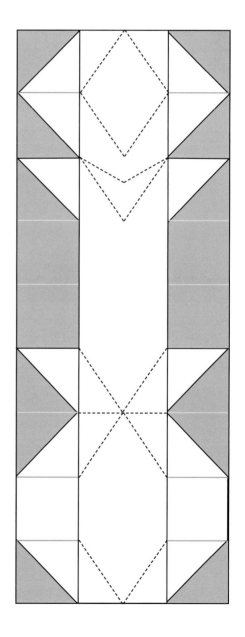

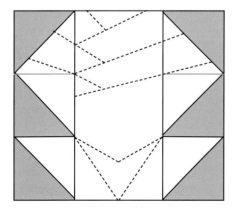

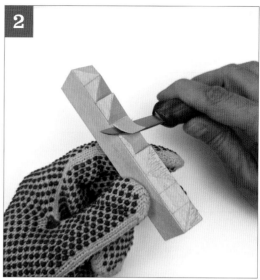

1 Apply the pattern. Flatten the block of wood by drawing vertical center lines on each face of the block, and then using your knife to remove the entire front and back corner between these vertical lines (see sidebar on page 32). Then, use a pencil and ruler to draw the pattern on the front and back of the wood. Note that the horizontal reference lines in the pattern run in ½" (1.3cm) intervals and the dotted pattern lines across the front can be drawn on as you go. The second pattern, showing just the rose bud and leaves, is used in step 14, but could also be used to carve a standalone rose bud.

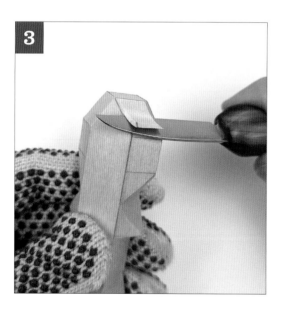

2 Rough out the shape. Use push cuts and V-cuts to remove the shaded areas from the pattern. To reduce the risk of breakage, work along each side from the top to the bottom. To remove the large areas on the sides of the stem, start by making a stop cut at the edge of the vase and carving down to it from the middle of the stem area. Then, make progressively larger V-cuts along the bottom of the leaf and carve up to it from the middle of the stem area. Once you have extended the cuts to the appropriate depth on the top and bottom this area, work to flatten the remaining area between them until the area along the stem is completely flat.

3 Angle the bottom of the vase. Use the pencil to draw the dotted pattern lines on the front and back of the bottom of the vase and a centerline along the outside edges of the bottom. Use your knife to completely flatten the area between the dotted pattern line and centerline along the base of the vase. Repeat on all four corners. When you are done, the bottom of the base will look like a diamond, or square shape.

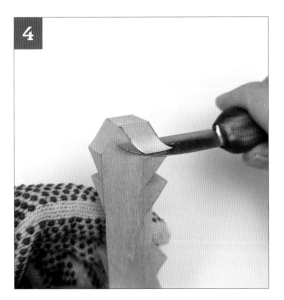

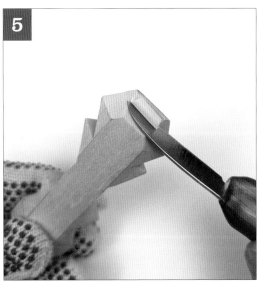

4 Angle the top of the rose. Draw the pattern lines on the front and back of the top of the rose and a centerline alongside of the outside edges of the top. Follow the same process as the previous step to similarly flatten the area between these two lines. Repeat the process on all four corners. When you are done, the top of the rose will look like a diamond, or a square shape, from the top.

5 Taper the top of the rose. Draw a centerline extending side-to-side across the top of the rose. Then, starting ¼" (6.4mm) down from the top, use push cuts to angle the front and back sides in toward the top of the rose, until you are left with a ridge across the top. Try to finish with a smooth flat surface on the front and back, tapering to the ridge on the top.

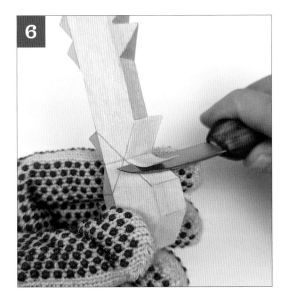

6 Shape the sides of the vase. Draw the pattern lines making an X shape across the front and back of the carving where the side of the vase pinches in toward the middle. Place a deep stop cut across one corner along the horizontal line, separating the top and bottom of the vase. Carve up and down to this stop cut until you have made a deep, angled V-cut across the sides, pinching into the center of the X. The area between the pattern lines and the center of the outside edges of the carving should be completely flat when you are done. Repeat on all four corners of the vase.

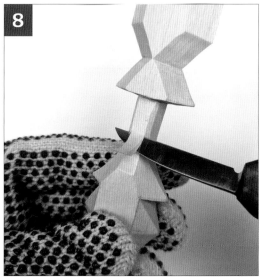

7 Begin shaping the stem. Draw the dotted pattern line making the V shape along the bottom of the leaves, and then draw a vertical centerline on each of the four sides of the stem area. Holding the carving upside down, narrow the stem by flattening each corner, until the area between the vertical centerline on either side is completely flat. This will leave you with a narrower square stem, with corners facing the front, back, and sides of the carving. When the sides of the stem are nearly flat, use the V-shaped pattern lines as a guide to angle the bottom of the leaves into the stem, rolling your knife slightly to create a smooth transition between the leaves and the stem. The angle of the bottom of the leaves should match the angle of the top of the vase, and then roll smoothly into the flat surfaces of the sides of the stem.

8 Narrow the stem. Continue to narrow the stem by once again drawing vertical center lines along each side of the stem and flattening each corner, until the surface between each centerline is completely flat. When you are finished, you will have an even narrower square-shaped stem, but with the flat surfaces of the stem once again facing the front, back, and sides of the carving.

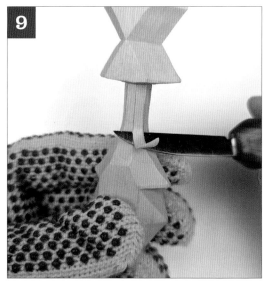

9 Finish the stem. Draw two vertical lines on each side of the stem, separating each face into three equal sections. Then, remove the four corners on the outside of the stem, flattening the area between the lines on either side of each corner. This will narrow the stem slightly and result in eight flat surfaces making up the stem instead of four. Next, narrow the front, sides, and edges of the leaves, rolling them smoothly into the eight sides of the stem. Finish with a deep rolling cut under each leaf to create a curved profile along the underside of the leaf as it meets the stem.

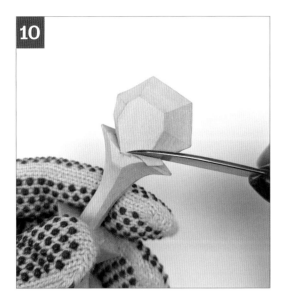

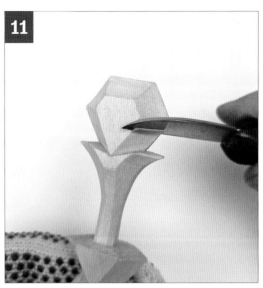

10 Separate the bud from the leaves. Draw the dotted pattern lines separating the top of the leaves from the bottom of the rose bud. Place a stop cut, followed by a V-cut along each of these lines, extending from the outside of the flower and ending at the center of the carving where the pattern lines meet.

11 Angle the bottom of the rose bud. Draw the remaining pattern lines showing the V shape on the bottom half of the front and back of the rose bud. Angle the bottom sides of the flowers from the outsides edge along these pattern lines and into the top of the flower. The angle of the bottom sides of the rosebud will match the angle of the top of the vase.

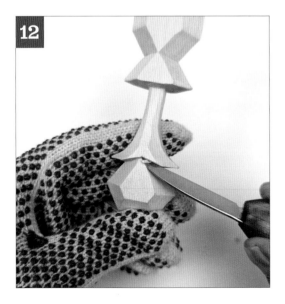

12 Separate the rose from the leaves. Remove a small triangle chip at the center of the base of the rose bud where it meets the leaves. Repeat on the other side of the carving.

13 Finish the leaves. Make a small V-cut extending along the top of the leaf on the right side across the center of the carving and over the left side. This will give the appearance of the leaf on the left being tucked under the leaf on the right. Repeat on the other side of the carving. Finally, use the tip of your knife to smooth the hard edges along the top of the leaves on all sides.

14 Carve the petals. Draw the pattern lines for the petals on the front and back of the rose as indicated in the bud pattern. Starting with the longest line on the bottom and working your way up, make V-cuts along each line. Start at the middle of the line with a single V-cut, and extend it forward across the front of the flower and back to the edges until the entire line has been cut. Cut the same line on the other side of the rose, and then move on to the next line up from the bottom, following a similar process to carve it on both sides. Take care to make cuts of similar depth, so that they line up where they meet and ensure that the lines on the front and back run into each other at the same point on the outside edges of the rose bud. Be careful as you near the top, as the last few cuts will involve carving directly into and across the grain.

15 Smooth the petals. Use the tip of your knife to smooth hard edges along the sides of the petals. Round off the hard corners between each petal along the outside edges of the rose.

Removing Pencil Marks

As you can see, I draw a lot of pencil lines as references as I go along in my carvings. This can result in a lot of marks that need to be removed before finishing. You can try erasers to remove these marks, but they often do more smudging than erasing. My preferred method for removing pencil marks is to shave them off with my knife. This keeps all surfaces looking clean and consistent. I also recommend drawing your lines on as lightly as possible to make them easier to remove, if needed. The lines you see in the pictures in this book are much darker than I would usually draw.

16 Flare the sides of the rose. Holding the carving upside down, make a rolling cut, pushing into the bottom side of the rose and rolling into the top of the leaf so that that bottom of the rose bud is curved as it meets the top of the leaf.

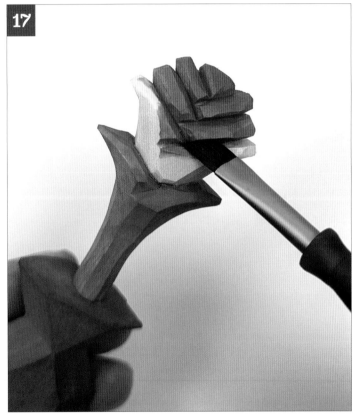

17 Paint and finish. Use a flat brush and watered-down (50% water, 50% paint) paints to paint the vase light blue, the stem and leaves green, and the rose red. Finish with a coat of Howard Feed-N-Wax.

Old Man in Wood

No matter how much I carve, I always come back to carving faces. The face is a subject that is both simple and complex, allowing for infinite practice, so it seems appropriate to close this book with one more face carving. Where the Simple Wood Spirit project earlier in the book was all about practicing with a V-tool, the goal of this project is to carve a face and hair with just a knife. Carving the facial features cleanly requires a keen awareness of where your knife edge is at all times as you carefully control the depth and angle of each cut. Carving the old man can be hairy at times, but the end result is a cheeky guy who wood be happy to share everything he nose with you. Seriously though, these are fun little carvings with lots of opportunity for customization . . . eye bet you can't carve just one!

Pattern

MATERIALS

- Basswood, 1" x 1" x 2" (2.5 x 2.5 x 5.1cm)
- FolkArt by Plaid acrylic paint: French Gray, Real Brown, Vintage White
- Howard Feed-N-Wax

TOOLS

- Carving knife
- Pencil
- Ruler
- Detail paintbrush
- Flat paintbrush

Photocopy at 100%.

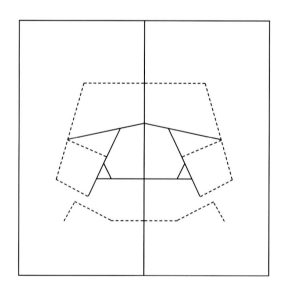

1 Apply the pattern. Use a pencil to draw the basic pattern for the nose and eyes are onto the carving. Note that the dotted lines will be drawn on as needed and represent approximate positions of the outline of the face and moustache. In this case, the pattern lines don't need to be exact, and you can experiment with widening or narrowing the nose, cheeks, or other facial features as desired.

2 Separate the nose. Make a stop cut along the bottom of the nose and carve up to it from below. Repeat until you have carved down to the width of the bottom of the nose. Then, make a large triangle cut to remove a deep chip on either side of the bottom of the nose. Make deep stop cuts on the top two sides of the triangle, and then slide the tip of your knife across the bottom to remove the chip. You may need to repeat this process a few times to deepen the cut.

3 Define the brow. Make stop cuts across the pattern lines for the brow line, and then carve up to them from about halfway down the nose. Make separate cuts on either side of the center ridge, taking care to make cuts of equal depth. Try to maintain a center ridge between your two cuts that runs vertically along the front of the nose, in line with the corner of the block of wood.

4 Round the sides and front. Begin by making a deep push cut, removing the hard corner of the block above the center of the nose. Then, continue on either side of this cut, smoothing and rounding the area above the brow line until the brow line is nearly removed. Remove the hard corners on either side of the wood block and continue rounding along the sides toward the front, including the area under the nose. The goal is to round the front and sides, so that the front and sides of the head are round with just the nose sticking out. You can choose to remove the hard corner on the back of the block, if desired as well.

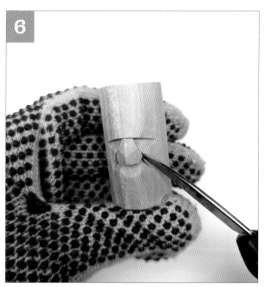

5 Carve the eye sockets. Redraw the pattern lines extending from the bottom corners of the nose up to the brow line. Make a small V-cut along this line on either side of the nose. Then, place deep stop cuts along the sides of the nose and the brow line, coming together at the point where the brow line meets the top of the nose. Carve up to this on both sides of the nose, starting about halfway down the nose, removing a large triangular area for the eye sockets.

6 Further define the nose. Run the tip of your knife downward along the side of the nose, starting at about the point where you carved up for the eye sockets. Remove a thin chip of wood behind the bottom corners of the nose and extending down along the smile lines created in step 1. This will make the nose more clearly stand out from the face. Then, use the tip of your knife to carve the sharp, outside corners off of both sides of the bottom of the nose.

7 Finish the nose. Begin by removing the hard corner from the tip of the nose. Then, deepen the angle of the nose starting about halfway up the nose and angling into the brow line. Do this evenly on the front and sides of the nose, making a slight rolling motion as you carve up the bridge of the nose. Next, lightly round the bottom edges of the nose and make small rolling cuts on the outside edges of the bottom to give an impression of nostrils. Finally, remove a small triangle chip from either side of the nose, just above where the smile lines meet the side of the nose.

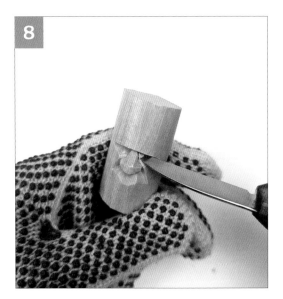

8 Finish the eyes. Remove another deep triangle chip from the eye area, in the corner where the nose meets the brow line. Then, use the tip of your knife to lightly smooth the edge of the brow line.

9 Carve the cheeks. Use the pencil to draw on the dotted pattern lines, defining the cheeks and forehead area. The cheek lines should angle upward at a 90-degree angle from the bottom of the smile lines and extend about ¼" (6.4mm) up toward the side of the head. The hairline is a horizontal line running about ½" (1.3cm) down from the top of the carving. The line connecting the cheeks to the forehead should angle inward, intersecting the outside edge of the brow line. Carve the bottom and side corners of the cheeks by placing a stop cut along each line, inserting the tip of the knife especially deeply at each corner. Then, carve into these stop cuts from inside the face area. Follow this process for the bottom sides of each cheek and the sides of the face leading up to the hairline.

Controlling Depth and Length of Cuts

A key to making clean cuts is to pay attention to the depth of your blade in the wood. In step 9, it is easy to over- or undercut the sides of the cheeks, resulting in messy cuts or unwanted lines extending outside of the face area. To avoid this, insert your knife at an angle, starting by inserting the tip deeply at the corner and angling the rest of the blade into the wood, until the cutting edge exits the wood right at the point where you want the cut to end. Paying attention to the depth and angle of the blade takes some practice but will result in nice clean cuts in the long run.

10 Carve the forehead. Use the tip of your knife to make a stop cut along the hairline. Then, remove a small triangle chip from the inside corners where the sides of the face meet the hairline. Carve up to the hairline from about halfway down the forehead, angling the forehead back into the hairline.

11 Finish the cheeks and face. Make a small triangle chip cut to remove the hard corners on the bottom and side corners of the cheeks. Then, gently smooth the hard edges making up the bottom and side of each cheek. Finally, use the tip of your knife to gently round the hard lines remaining along the sides of the head and across the hairline. Pay attention to the tip of your knife and avoid making unwanted cuts across the sides or top of the face while doing this.

12 Carve the eyebrows. Use your pencil to draw the upper border of the eyebrows. The eyebrows should start just above the outside edge of each eye area and angle up slightly, meeting in the center above the nose. Make small V-cuts along each of these lines to separate the eyebrows from the forehead. Then, remove a small triangle chip from the center of the eyebrows, with the tip of the triangle pointing down at the center of the nose. Finally, make three small V-cuts angling outward across each eyebrow.

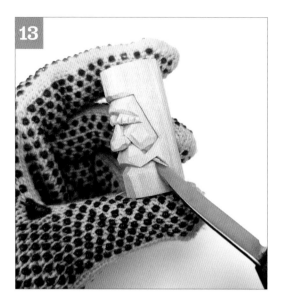

13 Define the moustache. Draw the dotted pattern lines for the shape of the moustache onto the carving. Make a horizontal V-cut across the front of the carving about ¼" (6.4mm) down from the nose, then extend it on both ends, angling down slightly. Make deep stop cuts widening the bottom of the moustache and meeting at the point where they point upward toward the cheeks. Then, slide the tip of your knife under this area to remove a large triangle chip from each side.

14 Finish the moustache. Carve up to the bottom of the moustache from below, rounding and flattening this area so that the moustache sticks out more than the wood beneath it. Then, use the tip of your knife to smooth the edges of the bottom of the moustache. Make a large triangle cut in the bottom of the center of the moustache. Then, make two small V-cuts along the bottom of both sides of the moustache. Deepen these by making small chip cuts at the point where each V-cut meets the bottom of the moustache.

15 Define the hair. Make a series of V-cuts around the head to separate the locks of hair. On each side, make one cut that angles toward the bottom to the side of the moustache and two cuts angling toward the top, along the sides of the head. On the top, make a series of four V-cuts that angle from right to left when looking at the carving, and four similar cuts along the bottom that angle from left to right. Extend each of these cuts and narrow them as the approach the border of the face. Widen each end of these cuts where they meet the side, top, or bottom of the carving.

16 Finish the hair. At the base of each V-cut on the bottom of the carving, add a stop cut directly into the center of the V shape. Then, carve into it from the left side of each cut to give an appearance of the hair turning back the other direction near the bottom. Follow a similar process to make angled cuts along each of the V-cuts at the top of the carving. Finally, carve the corner off of the top (or bottom) of each lock of hair running along the top or bottom of the carving.

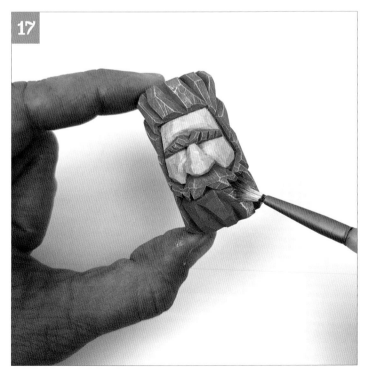

17 Paint and finish. Paint the hair, beard, and eyebrows of the carving with a watered-down (50% water, 50% paint) gray or another color of your choosing. Use a detail brush to carefully paint the area round the face and the eyebrows, and you can use a larger flat or round brush to finish the rest of the hair. Allow the paint to dry, and then lightly dry-brush over the painted areas with undiluted white paint. Leave the face and the sides and back of the carving unpainted. Finish with a coat of Howard Feed-N-Wax. For a simpler, more natural look, skip the painting and simply finish with Howard Feed-N-Wax.

Index

A

accessories, adding, 31-32
against the grain, carving, 72
Alligator, 62
animals,
    Alligator, 62
    Butterfly, 94
    Goldfish, 68
    Grumpy (or Happy) Cat, 80
    Hatching Chicks, 46
antiquing, 26-27
ash, 8

B

basswood, 8
birch, 8
blade awareness, 52
brushes, painting, 21
Butterfly, 94
butternut, 8

C

cactus, 40
carving communities, online, 30
cat, 80
cherry, 8
chicks, hatching, 46
chip cut, 19
clean cuts, with a V-tool, 60
compound, stropping, 14, 15

D

depth of cuts, 122
design, 79
detail knives, 67
dot eyes, 26

dry-brushing, 28

E

embossing tools, 22
eyelets, 31
eyes, painting, 25-26

F

finishing, 28-31
flat-plane carving, 44
flat surfaces, carving, 45
flattening, 32

G

Getting Started
    choosing a knife, 9-11
    introduction to wood, 8-9
    other materials and tools,
    11-13
    safety, 17-18
    sharpening, 13-16
    whittling, basic cuts, 18-19
gloves, carving, 17
gnomes, 88
Goldfish, 68
gouges, 12-13
grind, 10-11
    convex, 10-11
    flat, 10-11
    scandi, 10-11
Grumpy (or Happy) Cat, 80

H

happy eyes, 25
Hatching Chicks, 46

holding carving while painting,
22
Howard Feed-N-Wax, 28-29

K

knife
    blade material, 10
    choosing, 9-11
    cutting edge, 9
    detail tip, 10
    folding knives, 11
    grind, 10-11
    handle, 10
    length, 9
    sharpening, 13-16
    thickness, 9
    using as an eraser, 24

L

length of cuts, 122
limewood, 8
linden, 8

M

magnets, 32

N

northern basswood, 8

O

oil finishes, 31
Old Man in Wood, 126

P

paint, how to, 23-25
paintbrushes, 21
painting and finishing, 20-32
    adding accessories, 31-32
    antiquing and dry-brushing, 26-28
    finishing, 28-31
    painting, 20-26
palette, 21
paring cut, 18-19
pencil marks, removing, 117
people,
    Old Man in Wood, 118
    Super Simple Gnomes, 88
    Whittle People, 34
pine, 8
Pineapple, 102
plants,
    Rose in Vase, 110
    Simple Cactus, 40
poplar, 8
practice, carving, 37
projects
    Alligator, 62
    Butterfly, 94
    Goldfish, 68
    Grumpy (or Happy) Cat, 80
    Hatching Chicks, 46
    Old Man in Wood, 118
    Pineapple, 102
    Rose in Vase, 110
    Seashell, 74
    Simple Cactus, 40
    Simple Wood Spirit, 56
    Super Simple Gnomes, 88
    Whittle People, 34
push cut, 18

R

Rockwell Hardness Scale, 11
Rose in Vase, 110
roughout knives, 67

S

safety, 17-18
    safety equipment, 17-18
    safe practices, 18
sandpaper, 13, 15-16
saws, 13
scrap wood, practicing, 71
Seashell, 74
sharpening, 13-16
    sandpaper method, 15
    stropping, 14-15
    wood test, 13
sheaths, 17
Simple Cactus, 40
Simple Wood Spirit, 56
small pieces, carving, 48
social media groups, 30
southern basswood, 8
spray sealants, 30
steel hardness, 10, 11
stop cut, 19
Super Simple Gnomes, 88
supplies, purchasing, 12
symmetry, checking, 98

T

thumb guards, 17
tool storage, 18
tools, 9-13

U

U-gouges, 11, 12
undercutting, 49

V

V-cut, 19, 78
V-tools, 11-12
veiner, 12

W

walnut, 8
water-down paints, 22-23
wax finishes, 30
Whittle People, 34
whittling, basic cuts, 18-19
whittling, definition, 12
woodcarving, definition, 12
wood grain, understanding, 9
wood, introduction to, 8-9
wood, preparing, 9
wood, selecting, 8
wood breaking, how to deal, 39, 109
wood spirit, 56
wood test, sharpening, 13
wood treatment, 31

About the Author

Photo by Katie Young.

David Young lives in Michigan with his wife and three kids. A former math teacher, He now leads a team that designs and develops online courses. David's favorite subject was always geometry, which he appreciates for its patterns and symmetry. He started whittling in early 2019 when he stumbled on carving and found that it clicked for him in a way other hobbies hadn't. David learned from experienced carvers by reading their books and following along with their online videos. As an author and instructor, he focuses on designing simple carvings that use repeatable patterns and processes, making it easy to teach others how to recreate his designs. A regular contributor to *Woodcarving Illustrated*, David's first book is *Whittling on the Go*. He welcomes carvers trying his designs and sharing them on social media. You can find David on Instagram and YouTube **@dywoodcarving**.